STONEWALL

Who would ever have suspected that Thomas Jackson, a penniless orphan in West Virginia, would turn out to be a national hero? Certainly not friends from his childhood. They laughed about the time he fell in the river on the way to church, picked himself up, went on, and sat right through the services in his wet clothes. Later his classmates at West Point, watching him sweat through his recitations, doubted if he'd even graduate.

But Jackson was a fanatically determined man who ultimately was ranked one of America's most brilliant and indefatigable military leaders. Most surprising, however, is not that Stonewall was so successful in battle but that, with his particular assortment of personality traits, he should have become such a popular idol.

"A superior example of biographical writing. Facts, remarks and incidents are woven together into a picture of a complex and contradictory man."
—*School Library Journal* (starred review)

Jean Fritz
STONEWALL

with drawings by Stephen Gammell

Puffin Books

PUFFIN BOOKS
Published by the Penguin Group
Viking Penguin, a division of Penguin Books USA, Inc.,
40 West 23rd Street, New York, New York 10010, U.S.A.
Penguin Books Ltd, 27 Wrights Lane, London W8 5TZ, England
Penguin Books Australia Ltd, Ringwood, Victoria, Australia
Penguin Books Canada Ltd, 2801 John Street, Markham, Ontario, Canada L3R 1B4
Penguin Books (N.Z.) Ltd, 182–190 Wairau Road, Auckland 10, New Zealand

Penguin Books Ltd, Registered Offices: Harmondsworth, Middlesex, England

First published in the United States of America by G.P. Putnam's Sons, 1979
Published in Puffin Books 1989
1 3 5 7 9 10 8 6 4 2

LIBRARY OF CONGRESS CATALOGING-IN-PUBLICATION DATA
Fritz, Jean.
Stonewall / by Jean Fritz ; with drawings by Stephen Gammell.   p.   cm.
Reprint. Originally published: New York : Putnam, c1979.
Summary: A biography of the brilliant Southern general who gained
the nickname Stonewall by his stand at Bull Run during the Civil War.
ISBN 0-14-032937-4
1. Jackson, Stonewall, 1824–1863—Juvenile literature.
2. Generals—United States—Biography—Juvenile literature.
3. Confederate States of America. Army—Biography—Juvenile
literature. 4. United States. Army—Biography—Juvenile
literature. 5. United States—History—Civil War, 1861–1865—
Campaigns—Juvenile literature. [1. Jackson, Stonewall,
1824–1863. 2. Generals. 3. United States—History—Civil War,
1861–1865.] I. Gammell, Stephen, ill. II. Title.
E467.1.J15F74 1989   973.7'3'0924–dc19   [B] [92]   89-3607

Printed in the United States of America
by R. R. Donnelley & Sons Company, Harrisonburg, Virginia
Set in Bembo

For
Fran and Jerry Jacobs

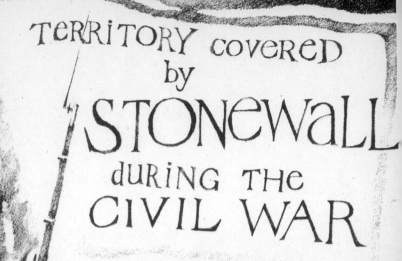

TERRITORY COVERED by STONEWALL DURING THE CIVIL WAR

ALLEGHENY MTS.

WEST VIRGINIA

McDOWELL

STAUNTON

LEXINGTON

NORTH
SOUTH

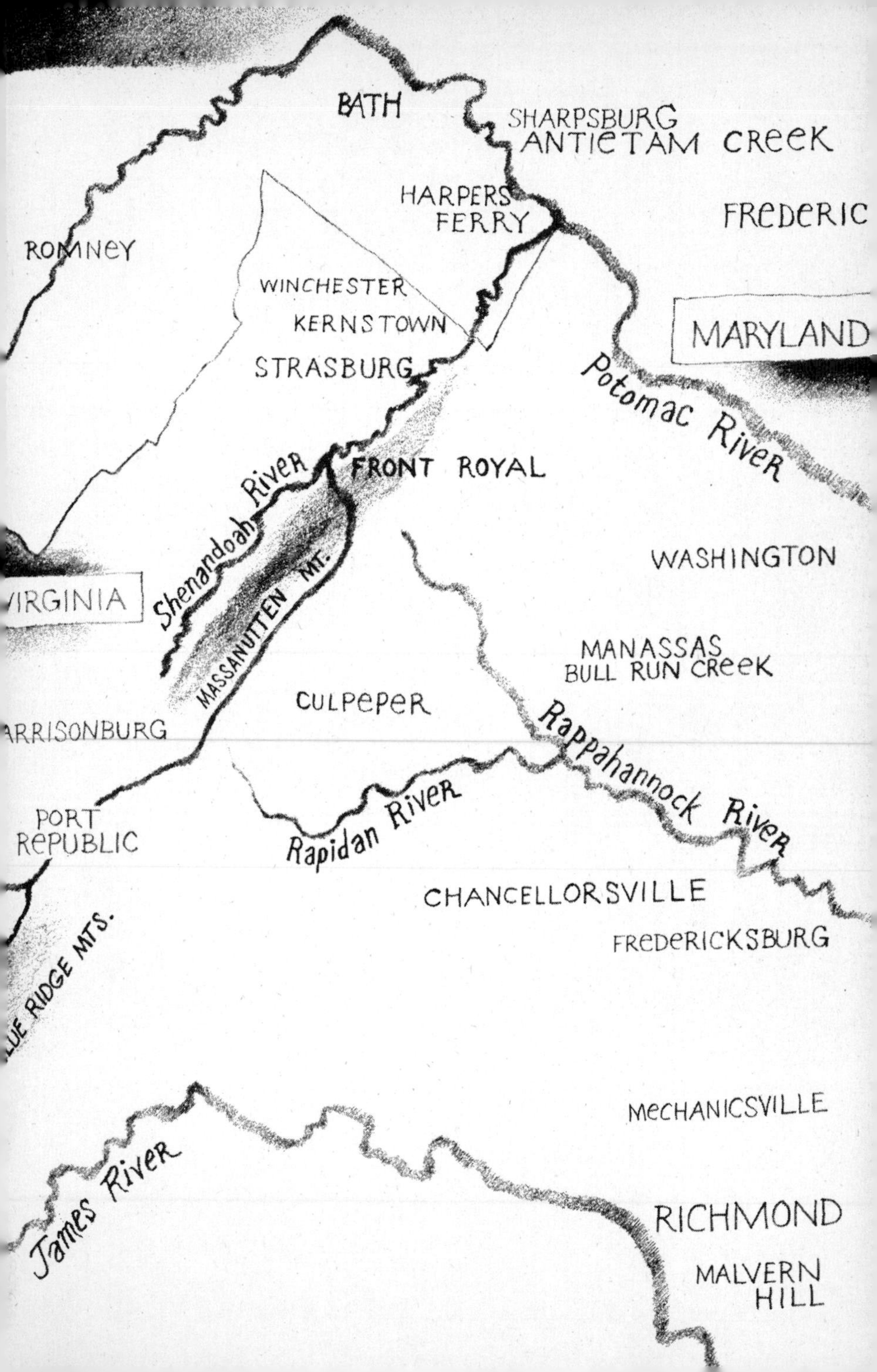
BATH
SHARPSBURG
ANTIETAM CREEK
HARPERS FERRY
FREDERIC
ROMNEY
WINCHESTER
KERNSTOWN
STRASBURG
MARYLAND
Potomac River
FRONT ROYAL
Shenandoah River
MASSANUTTEN MT.
WASHINGTON
VIRGINIA
MANASSAS
BULL RUN CREEK
CULPEPER
ARRISONBURG
Rappahannock River
PORT REPUBLIC
Rapidan River
CHANCELLORSVILLE
FREDERICKSBURG
LUE RIDGE MTS.
MECHANICSVILLE
James River
RICHMOND
MALVERN HILL

One

*T*OM *Jackson was born in 1824, but he wasn't sure if it had been on January 20th or the 21st.* The records had been lost, yet no one supposed that made any difference. Not in Tom's case. His birth date wasn't likely to find its way into print. Although the Jacksons were a leading family in northwestern Virginia, their luck seemed to have petered out when it came to young Tom. No one in the 1840's, looking over the young men in the area, would have picked Tom Jackson as one who was likely to go far in the world. Certainly no one could have imagined a set of circumstances that could turn him into a hero.

His bad luck began when he was two years old and his father died, leaving behind such a string of debts that his mother had to sell all their property, including the nice brick house in Clarksburg in which Tom had been born. So Tom, his baby sister, Laura, his older brother, Warren, and his mother, Julia, were suddenly without a place to live and without money to live on. Mrs. Jackson could have split up the family and sent the children to different relatives, but she wouldn't do that. Instead she accepted a one-room cottage provided out of a local charity fund. To make money, she took in sewing and taught school.

But it was a difficult life and after four years when Mr. Blake Woodson offered to marry her, she was inclined to accept. The Jacksons were against it. Mr. Woodson had a poor record in business, they said, and Julia would be worse off than she was now. But Julia Jackson went right ahead and married Mr. Woodson, and when he took a job in a neighboring county, she and the children moved with him. Hardly had they settled, however, when more bad luck set in. Julia became so sick that she couldn't care for her children. In spite of all she'd done to keep her family together, she had to send Warren, Tom, and Laura away to live with relatives. Tom saw his mother only once again. A few months later when it was clear that his mother would not live, Tom was taken for a last visit. She died while he was there.

So at the age of seven Tom was an orphan with only sad memories to look back on. Indeed, those years between his father's death and his mother's had been so painful that he didn't like to talk about them even when he was grown up. Yet there was no erasing them; they were a hard knot at the very root of his character. Young as he was, he knew that his father had failed his family. This was hard to bear because the Jacksons were used to success. After all, there had been a congressman in the family and a number of judges, and a cousin had married President Madison's sister-in-law right in the White House. Even Tom's grandmother had been worth talking about. People still told stories about Eliza Jackson who'd been six feet tall and could handle a rifle as well as any man.

And now they talked about Tom's father who'd had a promising reputation as a lawyer and had thrown it away, gambling at cards and signing his name recklessly to other men's debts. It wasn't easy for Tom to hear his father discussed and he hadn't liked watching his mother work so hard when other women in the Jackson family had slaves to wait on them. Tom couldn't have put his feelings into words then, nevertheless they were there: sometime he would make up for all that had gone wrong in those years. He'd bring credit back to his branch of the family. He'd be a person who was noticed.

At the moment, however, Tom had to think about his life right now. While Warren had gone to live with his mother's relatives, Tom and Laura had been sent twenty miles south of Clarksburg to their bachelor uncle, Cummins Jackson, who owned one of the biggest and prettiest farms in western Virginia. Standing on the front porch of his farmhouse, a person might imagine he was on an island. Freeman's Creek and the West Fork River met and curved in a half circle before the property, with wooded hills on the other side. Cummins had built a gristmill and a sawmill on that curve of water and people from miles around came to use his mills.

The rumble of wagon wheels, the slip-slopping of water, the buzzing of machinery formed a background music for all the farmwork.

At the center of all this busy-ness was Cummins himself, a large, boisterous man noted for his strength, his scrappiness, and his popularity. People said Cummins could carry a barrel of flour under each arm without even raising a sweat. And if he wanted a drink of cider, he'd just heave up a barrel, tip it to his lips, and drink from the bunghole. As for his scrappiness, he didn't waste time bickering with people he differed with; he went straight to court. He was like a juggler the way he handled so many lawsuits at the same time. He did what he wanted, regardless of anyone's rights, then sat back and let the charges fly. (Once he built a dam which the neighbors contended was an obstruction.) But let anyone else interfere with Cummins' rights and "by hevins," as he'd say, he'd have the law on him in a minute. Of course he made enemies this way but he had more than enough friends to offset them. He had helped too many neighbors and employed too many boys who needed work not to be appreciated. Indeed, unless someone got in his way, Cummins was big-hearted, open-handed, and fun-loving. Tom could not help but warm up to him.

In return Cummins liked Tom. More important, he seemed to understand that although Tom was a child, he took himself too seriously to be treated as a child. So Cummins talked to Tom as if he were an equal, suggesting chores that had to be done and asking advice. Tom responded and soon became involved in the cycle of work that followed the seasons on the farm. In the winter he helped the hired hands cut down poplar trees; then he'd hitch up a team of oxen and drag the logs to the sawmill. In the summer he worked in the corn and wheatfields. In the spring he tapped maple trees and sheared sheep. He took pride in those maple trees for they were his special project and on the first warm days he imagined that the trees waited for him to come around and check them.

But life was not all work. Cummins Jackson would be the last person to deny anyone a good time. Tom went fox hunting with his uncle. He fished and trapped. He hollowed out a log once to make himself a canoe. He fashioned fiddles out of cornstalks. And when Joe Lightburn, a boy his age, moved to the neighborhood, he took time out to make friends. Tom had never been much of a talker, but with Joe it came easy. They exchanged views on all sorts of subjects, on religion, for instance. (Tom went to church but admitted he didn't understand it too well.) They talked about war and old-time heroes, like Napoleon, Washington, and Francis Marion, the "Swamp Fox," who had been so wily in outwitting the British in the Revolutionary War. Joe had a book about Marion and the boys never tired of studying his tactics. And what about slavery? Tom said he felt sorry for the race but Joe said it wasn't practical to feel that way. "Do you want to black your own boots?" he asked. Tom said he wouldn't mind. He'd only do it on Sundays anyway and in winter he wouldn't bother.

Of course Tom attended school whenever it was in session but that wasn't often. One year he went for thirty-nine days and another year for a total of two months. Because Tom was an orphan, his uncle didn't have to pay for him; his tuition came out of a school fund for poor children. Tom learned slowly but studied hard, knowing all the time, however, that if he wanted more than a local education there would be no money for it. The Jacksons would help him in other ways but he knew he couldn't expect money.

Tom regarded this period of his life as happy and carefree, but some of his Clarksburg relatives considered it entirely too carefree. Cummins Jackson's farm, they said, was no place to bring up children, especially now that there were no women except slaves on the place. Cummins' mother (Tom's step-grandmother) had died since Tom had moved in and Cummins' sister had married and gone away. The relatives had already transferred Laura to a family in Parkersburg and now they clucked in disapproval at the rough, male life that Tom led with his uncle. Why, Cummins didn't even go to church, they pointed out. But let there be a log rolling or a house raising or a shindig of any kind and Cummins would be there and Tom with him. Some of these affairs might start out sober enough but they seldom ended up that way. And horse races! Cummins' own farm was the center for horse racing. Men from all over the county came to the farm and bet and drank and smoked and swore and spit and carried on the way men did at horse races. And where would Tom be? Well, he'd be on the back of one of his uncle's horses, riding as hard as he could ride. He didn't care much for racing, he said, but anyone could see that he liked to win. Moreover, he insisted he'd ride any time his uncle asked him. His uncle had been good to him and no matter what anyone said, he intended to stick to him through thick and thin.

But Tom's Uncle Brake decided to put an end to this kind of loose living. He'd take Tom home with him and bring him up right. A boy needed a strong hand, he said. So Tom went to his Uncle Brake's and his Aunt Polly's, but as it turned out, his uncle's hand wasn't strong enough to hold him. Tom never told what happened at his uncle's house but one day he left. Without a word, he just walked out. He appeared at his Uncle John's house in Clarksburg. "I've quit Uncle Brake," he announced. "We don't agree," and though his Uncle John's family tried to reason with him, Tom was firm. "No, I've quit," he said. He walked twenty miles to his Uncle Cummins and there he stayed.

People smiled that such a young boy—not yet in his teens—could have such strong notions and do such odd things. A neighbor told of an instance when Tom was walking by with a string of fish he'd caught. One was a prize three-foot pike.

"I'll give you a dollar for that fish," the neighbor said.

Tom shook his head. "I've already promised it. Mr. Kester is going to pay me fifty cents for it."

He began with what might seem like simple rules. Tell the truth. Don't break promises. Do what you set out to do. In actual practice following these rules without any allowance for exceptions might lead to odd behavior, but if he broke a rule, he'd be slipping and how would he be sure he could pull himself back? All he knew was that in order to feel safe, he had to find rules and then, no matter what, he had to stick to them.

In a few years he would find the most important rule of all, the guideline for his life. "You may be whatever you resolve to be." The words surfaced from that hard knot inside that had never left him nor would ever leave.

"But I offered you a dollar," the neighbor pointed out.

Tom explained that he'd made a bargain with Mr. Kester, the gunsmith. He'd sell him all the fish he caught of a certain size at fifty cents each.

"A dollar and a quarter?" the neighbor offered.

No. Tom wouldn't go back on his word. What was more, when Mr. Kester offered to pay more money for such a big fish, Tom wouldn't take it.

Then there was another story about the time young Tom fell into the river on the way to church. And what did he do? He got himself out of the river, went right on to church as if nothing had happened, and sat through the whole service in hi dripping clothes.

There was something amusing and innoce about such stubborn single-mindedness in a you boy and people supposed that the day would co when Tom would look back and laugh with tl at these stories.

But that day never came. The stories that p told about Tom Jackson's childhood were jus those they told about him as an adult. And he saw anything amusing in them. But then To not like other people and didn't study their ior to learn how to act. He decided very ea he had to find rules for his life and ther them strictly. He wasn't going to let life pen to him. He wasn't going to be like and slip carelessly into errors and from ruin. He was going to be in charge.

🌿🌿 Two

*A*LTHOUGH *Tom wanted to be a success, he* had no towering ambition to be a success at anything in particular. Of course for someone who was starting out with nothing, opportunities were limited. He couldn't be a farmer without land or a businessman without owning a business or a doctor or a lawyer without more education. But first, he had to be independent and even that was hard.

When Tom was thirteen, his brother Warren, who was three years older, decided that the two of them ought to go west as so many people were doing and seek their fortunes there. Warren had heard that a person could make good money by chopping down trees on islands in the Ohio and Mississippi Rivers and then selling the timber to steamboat captains. So they went to the Ohio and when they couldn't find any islands handy they went on to the Mississippi. There they were luckier.

Setting up camp on one of the many wooded islands, they began chopping and, just as Warren had predicted, they had no trouble selling. What Warren had not foreseen were the hardships they'd be up against: the isolation, the dampness, the difficulty of providing for themselves. As for their fortunes, they made enough money for each of them to buy a trunk. That was at least a small step forward. A man with a trunk was a man of property, whether or not he had anything to put into it. But at the end of six months the boys took sick, got rid of their trunks, which were too awkward to transport, and went home. Tom regained his health quickly, but the exposure had been too much for Warren. He developed tuberculosis and died three years later.

Tom, the only male member left of his immediate family, would feel his responsibilities even more keenly, but that moment still lay ahead. Right now he was trying to figure out how to make money at home. For a couple of months he joined the routine at the farm, and then Uncle Cummins found him a job with a crew building a turnpike through western Virginia. It was only a summer job, and though Tom liked it well enough, he didn't foresee a future in it.

What else could he do? At sixteen, he'd finished school, so he decided to try his hand at being a teacher. He boarded with a neighboring family and took on a one-room school with greased paper for windows and split logs for benches. The children paid three cents a day for tuition and in return learned not only the regular subject matter but some of Tom's rules. They were expected to improve both their penmanship and their morals as they copied from the blackboard. "A man of words and not of deeds," Tom wrote, "is like a garden full of weeds."

There were no light moments or relaxation in Tom Jackson's classroom but at the end of the day when he went home to the family he boarded with, he dropped some of his formality, especially when he was alone with the children. Often stiff and quiet with adults, in the company of children Tom sometimes even allowed himself to be silly. One evening before the fire Tom happened to make a funny face and he was done for. Every night the children squealed for more and funnier faces and generally Tom obliged. Serious schoolteacher by day, he was for four months a funny face-maker at night, and then the school term was over. He was no farther ahead nor would he be if he taught there the rest of his life.

What next?

Uncle Cummins suggested public office, so in the spring of 1841, although Tom was only seventeen years old, he ran for constable against a man named Richard Hall. The election did not arouse much interest for only seventeen votes were cast. Richard Hall received twelve votes and Tom Jackson five, yet for some reason unexplained in the records, Tom became constable. Perhaps Cummins was at work behind the scenes; in any case, Tom assumed office on June 8.

His primary duty was to collect debts, or rather try to collect them. This was a tricky business. If the debtor didn't want to pay, all he had to do was to run inside his house and he'd be legally safe. The constable was not allowed to unlatch a window or open a door of the debtor's house to press charges or to remove property in payment for the debt. Nor could the constable take a man's horse in payment if the man was on his horse.

But once Tom did manage to outwit a stubborn debtor. Knowing that the man was out on his horse, Tom hid in the shadows of the stable. As soon as the debtor returned and dismounted in order to enter the stable, Tom jumped out and grabbed the horse. There was a scuffle but in the end the debtor handed over the $10 he owed.

Tom won that case but he didn't like the job. He just couldn't seem to find a career that suited him. In later years when his religion had firmed up he would look back on this bleak period and say that God was at work behind the scenes all the time. For didn't opportunity come knocking just when he needed it most? In the spring of 1842 Weston's local congressman, Samuel Hays, announced that there was a vacancy at the United States Military Academy at West Point to be filled from his district. The academy offered four years of higher education free and a career in the army if that's what a graduate wanted. And by this time Tom Jackson knew that whatever he did, he needed an education. And here was his chance. Free.

Four candidates in the Weston area applied for the vacancy: Tom, Joe Lightburn, Gibson Butcher, and Johnson Camden. Tom asked a lawyer friend to coach him for the examination that would determine who would receive the appointment. Tom's only consolation was that the other boys had been as poorly educated as he'd been. Nevertheless, when the results of the examination were announced, Gibson Butcher won the appointment.

Still, as it turned out, opportunity had not quite finished with Tom. Gibson had been gone only a few weeks when suddenly he was back, knocking on the Jacksons' door. He'd quit West Point, he told Tom and Cummins. And glad of it. Never would he agree to lead a life like that. Duties every minute of the day. Schedules. Routine. Drilling. It was all "Yes, sir" and saluting and being on time and making up your bed just so and polishing your sword and your boots and your buckles and heaven knew what else. *Besides* studying, Gibson said. French! Philosophy! Mineralogy! Gibson reeled off the courses as if even their names were hard to believe. He couldn't see how anyone in his right mind would be interested, but if Tom wanted to try for his place, he was welcome.

Tom went to work. With Cummins' help, he secured letters of recommendation from some of the most influential men in the county. Then with his wide felt constable hat flat on top of his head and his saddlebags over his shoulders, he took the stagecoach to Washington, D. C. On June 17th he presented himself to Congressman Hays who in turn sent him for an interview with the Secretary of War. Certainly there was nothing promising in either Tom's record or his looks—a boy of middling height with conspicuously large feet who walked as if he were battling a wind. Yet there was a kind of concentrated force about his personality, an intensity to his blue eyes that made a person want to give him a chance. In any case, Tom was allowed to proceed to West Point with the understanding that he would take entrance examinations soon after his arrival.

Tom knew the history of West Point and its reputation for turning out leaders. He knew that many of the students came from aristocratic families and had received first class educations, yet he could hardly have been prepared for his first view of the academy itself. Standing on a cliff overlooking the Hudson River, the buildings were bleak and stern looking. With just one look, a person could see that this was a place of testing, a place of trials and ordeals where strong men were singled out and weak ones were doomed. Walking on to the grounds of the academy, Tom was so awed by the enormity of what he was undertaking that he probably never noticed the three students standing by the barracks. But they noticed him, not only his countrified appearance but the dramatic determination stamped on his face and confirmed in his walk. "That fellow looks as if he's come to stay," Dabney Maury, a fellow Virginian, laughed, but later when Maury tried to be sociable, Tom cut him off. He was in no condition yet to make friends. He had exams to take and already he was planning what he would say in Weston if he should fail. "Well," he'd say, "if you'd been there and found the exams as hard as I did, you would have failed too."

Fortunately Tom didn't have to use the excuse. He passed his exams—barely, but at least when he went home on his first vacation he could describe the ordeal without apology. The worst had been English grammar. He'd had only three weeks to learn the whole of it. "Oh, I tell you," he said, "I had to work hard."

Friends, who had already heard the horrors of West Point from Gibson Butcher, wondered if Tom would go back.

Why, he wouldn't fail to go back, Tom said. "I'm going to make a man of myself if I live. What I will do, I can do."

Yet his will power was strained to its limits that first year at West Point. Not only was he poorly prepared, he was a slow learner. Yet he was so determined that after lights were required to be out at night, Tom worked on by the glow from his coal fire, sometimes until morning. In order to remember what he learned, he developed the habit of staring at a wall and going over in his mind the entire lesson.

But however determined he was, no one watching him struggle would have guessed that Tom Jackson ("The General" as they called him) could have survived four years at West Point. Indeed he could hardly get through a recitation. When called on to answer a question or solve a problem, Tom sweated so profusely his classmates joked that one day he would drown them all.

Yet inch by inch Tom pulled himself through. Near the bottom of his class at the end of his first year (fifty-first in a class of seventy-two), he rose to seventeenth by the end of his senior year, and his classmates, who had grown fond of him, said it was a pity there wasn't a fifth year at West Point. Tom would have graduated top man.

The discipline at West Point suited Tom. A rule maker himself, he operated best in a system built on rules. Indeed his experience here seemed to prove not only that his rules worked but the principle of following rules worked. He even developed rules to govern his body. Having suffered from a nervous stomach since boyhood, Tom decided at West Point that his digestion would be improved if he kept his alimentary canal absolutely straight at all times. So he stood erect and sat erect, even on the most informal occasions, even when alone. Then there was the matter of his sweating. He imagined that he sweated more on one side of his body than the other, so to improve the circulation and release the sweat on the drier side, he made it a rule to massage that side regularly. He must have known, of course, that his classmates, though friendly to him, thought him an odd fellow, but this disturbed him not at all.

Still, however strict he was in observing rules, Tom did not have a perfect record in conduct. In his freshman year he received a demerit for being late at morning parade and another for being inattentive at drill. Once he appeared at inspection in a torn coat, another time with unpolished shoes. Two more demerits. He pulled the trigger on his musket once before he should have and arrived at church later than he should have. But none of these errors was deliberate, he said. The only time he ever did anything wrong deliberately was once when he was out of bounds; he stepped behind a tree so an officer wouldn't see him.

But if Tom had high standards for himself, he held others to the same standards. Later in life he would refuse to enter a store if he thought the merchant was dishonest. He wouldn't attend a church whose minister had violated a principle Tom felt was important. Often he stopped whatever he was doing to scold someone for cursing.

But sometimes he overreacted to other people's behavior. So at West Point when a cadet secretly substituted his dirty musket for Tom's clean one, Tom was so outraged that he wanted to press charges and have that cadet court-martialed. Tom's friends pointed out that was too severe a punishment for a minor piece of mischief. After all, the cadet was like Tom, an orphan who had to work hard. Tom remained unmoved. Justice should be done, he said. In the end he did yield to his friends' arguments but he saw no reason to forgive the cadet.

When it became obvious that Tom would indeed graduate from West Point, he began speaking frankly of his desire to make a name for himself. Never before and never again would he admit his ambitions so openly as he did just before he left West Point and in the years that immediately followed. It was to his sister Laura (now Mrs. Arnold of Beverly, Virginia) that he confessed most often. He wanted "to acquire a name," he said; "to distinguish himself." And when in the spring of his senior year the United States declared war on Mexico, he recognized that here was his chance if only the war would last long enough for him to get in it. For a West Point officer rank was everything, he pointed out to Laura, and of course there was no faster way to achieve it than on a battlefield.

Tom needn't have worried. He graduated from West Point on June 30, 1846, and on July 22nd he received his orders to report for active duty. Brevet (or honorary) Lieutenant Thomas J. Jackson he was now, having added the "J" (for his father, Jonathan) at West Point to distinguish him from another Thomas Jackson, also a cadet.

On September 24th twenty-two-year-old Tom arrived at Point Isabel, Texas, ready for action. But on that very day Mexico and the United States agreed to an eight-week truce. If he was to fight at all, he'd just have to wait.

"If only I could be in one battle," Tom sighed.

Three

*A*LTHOUGH *the United States gave many rea-*
sons for fighting the Mexican War, the
main purpose was to acquire the territories
of California and New Mexico after Mexico had
refused to sell them. Many Americans protested
that such a war was immoral but this would not
likely have bothered the conscience of a West Point
graduate. After four years of reading about battles,
most graduates welcomed a chance to see the real
thing. Certainly while the army was preparing for
invasion, Thomas Jackson was impatient. He looked
for officers who'd been in battle. What was it like?
he asked. How did a person feel?

It would be more than six months before Tom
would finally get to Mexico and find out for himself. He took part in the seige of the city of Vera
Cruz and was sick to his stomach when he saw his
first corpse. He soon became used to the sight of
death, however, and was startled to find that he
actually thrived on danger. He enjoyed a battle;
fighting made him feel stronger and more capable

than he'd ever felt in his life. Afterward, he reported proudly to Laura that a cannon ball "came in about five steps of me." It had not occurred to him to be afraid. He just wished he'd been in heavier fighting. Perhaps next time, he thought. Instead, after the fall of Vera Cruz, Tom was pulled out of action entirely. While the army marched ahead to Mexico City, Tom was left on garrison duty in a city along the way. He was not only disappointed, he was "mortified," he said. From April until July he fretted and fussed until at last, as a result of his petitions, he was allowed to rejoin the main core of the advancing army.

In the next month Jackson participated in two skirmishes and came away with a Mexican saber. He had still not had a real chance to prove himself; he had not been anyplace where his action might have changed the course of a battle. For that he would have to wait until the army reached Chapultepec.

A castlelike fortress on top of a high hill, Chapultepec was a combination summer palace and military college in which the Mexicans took special pride. Chapultepec would have to be taken before the army could proceed to the capital, Mexico City. After two days of fighting, Lieutenant Jackson, under the command of Colonel Trousdale, was ordered to a position where he was supposed to prevent the arrival of reinforcements and to cut off a Mexican retreat. But some Mexican reinforcements had already arrived and stationed themselves on the hill where the Americans wanted to be. Jackson and his unit were stuck behind a wide ditch and were under heavy fire. They had two cannon but they were useless unless they could be moved across the ditch. And that did not seem possible. Already Colonel Trousdale had been wounded, most of the American horses had been shot down, and Jackson's men lay on the ground and refused to budge.

Suddenly Thomas Jackson took fire. When had he ever recognized that anything was impossible? With bullets raining all around him, he sprang before his men and began pacing up and down. "There is no danger!" he shouted. "See, I am not hit. Follow me!" His men thought he was crazy; certainly they didn't move. So Jackson, himself, with the help of one sergeant, began dragging a cannon across the ditch. Even Jackson's superior officers decided the situation was hopeless and sent word for him to retire. Jackson insisted that it was not hopeless and begged to stay. If he had one additional company, he said, he could wipe out that enemy unit. He was so convincing that not only a company but a brigade was sent to him and in short order the Americans were across the ditch, the cannon was moved, and the enemy was routed. Thomas Jackson had made his mark.

When asked if he'd been afraid, Jackson's reply was a resounding "No!" His only fear, he said, was that he would not meet enough danger to make his "conduct conspicuous." But on that score he must have been satisfied, for on official reports his name was singled out. He was referred to as "the brave

Lieutenant Jackson," "the gallant Lieutenant," and was commended for his devotion, his industry, and his talent. Even the commanding general, Winfield Scott, complimented him in person before a large company, and although Jackson was embarrassed, as always, at any attention, he nevertheless treasured the praise. Perhaps more important than the praise, however, was the discovery of his own strength. In battle he was not just the dogged worker he'd been at West Point, worrying about which side of him sweated more. He was a man ablaze. It was as if that knot of ambition were released with such sudden force, he transcended himself. He became the kind of man he dreamed of being, not the kind he normally found himself.

It was an interesting discovery but not likely to be of much immediate use, for after the action at Chapultepec, the American army marched into Mexico City and the fighting was over. Although Jackson had attained an honorary rank of major and had been a hero for a day, there was little hope of building on this record now. Indeed service in the peacetime army normally offered little excitement and almost no chance for spectacular advancement.

Still, for the next nine months he was stationed in Mexico City in an environment so exotic, so different from anything he had experienced that he couldn't help but be stimulated. He was entertained by prominent Spanish families, he learned the language, and he saw the sights. Generally after dinner he took a ride on the Paseo, a wide road with a

33

beautiful fountain in the center, where fashionable people promenaded. He seemed to enjoy every-thing—the tropical flowers, the fresh fruit, the custom of eating breakfast in bed. For a while at least he must have enjoyed the company of a particular lady, for he wrote to Laura that he might decide "to make my life more natural by sharing it with some amiable señorita."

But despite his social life and brief romance (if that's what it was), Tom was still a man who lived by rules and needed purposes to work for. Yet with West Point behind him and the Mexican War over, he was without any immediate or demanding goals. He could, of course, expect the regular advancements that came to army officers, but this was hardly a big enough outlet for his ambition. He may not have been aware of the vacuum left in his life, yet perhaps it was no coincidence that he was beginning to consider religion more seriously. His company commander at Point Isabel and again at Mexico City, Captain Francis Taylor, prodded him about it. How could a man, he asked, who had such a rigid sense of right and wrong be so vague about the Bible? Why had he never joined a church? Didn't it bother him that he didn't even know whether he'd been baptized?

It wasn't that religion didn't interest Tom. How could he help but be attracted to the Bible with all its rules? He did attend church but only out of a sense of duty which probably went back to the influence of his mother. All his life Tom had been haunted by the memory of his last visit with her.

On her deathbed she had prayed aloud for Tom, committing his soul to the care of God. He had been awed at the time and had often worried if he shouldn't make some commitment in return. He wasn't ready for that yet, but under the guidance of Captain Taylor, he was becoming more and more convinced that God was really in charge of the world. Even in charge of what happened to him. Perhaps a person who wanted to run his own life should join forces with God. On the other hand, perhaps he should think less of getting ahead. Perhaps God didn't like a person to be ambitious for himself. He remembered that miserable period when he'd been left behind on garrison duty. Maybe that was God's doing, he wrote Laura. It may have been God's way of punishing him for his "excessive ambition." But when God kept him alive and unhurt at Chapultepec, Thomas Jackson decided it was time to learn more about God.

Being Thomas Jackson, he was, of course, thorough, establishing a regular routine of prayer and Bible reading. Since the Catholic Church was close at hand, he began studying it, interviewing the archbishop and visiting a monastery. In the end he decided that he needed a plainer form of worship so he settled on the Protestant Church. But what denomination? That required still more time and study.

In the midst of this religious activity, he was transferred to Fort Hamilton, New York. Actually, he seemed to be in something of a turmoil. His stomach, no matter how straight he held his alimentary canal, was troubling him again and if God was in charge of him, he reasoned, God must also be in charge of his stomach. So Tom was obviously being punished again. For what? Past sins, he said— whatever they were. So he prayed and put himself on a diet of stale unbuttered bread and lean meat. No tea, coffee, or stimulants of any kind. And he exercised. Fast walks accompanied by leaps and arm-whirlings. He worried about his arms. One arm, he decided, was heavier than the other so he developed the habit of thrusting the heavy one up in the air at regular intervals. This way the blood would run back into the body, he figured, and lighten the arm.

And, of course, everything (his eating, his sleeping, his exercises) had to be done according to an unwavering schedule. All of this gave him a reputation as a peculiar person, yet he had friends. They might find it hard to imagine him as a hero even for a day but they were nevertheless fond of him. Still, they had to accept him on his own terms. If they invited him to dinner, they knew he would bring his stale bread and lean meat in a paper bag. And they knew that he would watch the clock and no matter what was going on, he would leave at the exact minute that would get him into bed on time. Once some friends tried to trick him into staying late. They persuaded him to join a game which was at its height when his normal departure time came around. They thought he would be too interested to leave and too polite to break up a game. But no, right on the dot as usual, Tom got up and excused himself. If he broke a rule once, he might do it again and then where would he be?

Tom's religion gave him the most demanding rules of all. On April 29, 1849, he was baptized. He made it clear he was not *joining* the church because he had still not decided which denomination he wished to belong to. However, his baptism was a total commitment of faith. All his discipline was directed now to elevating his character so he might better fulfill the will of God. "Rather than wilfully violate the known will of God," he said, "I would forfeit my life." Yet whether it was God's will or not, that knot of ambition had not lessened. Sometimes he subdued or disguised it; sometimes he let it creep out in the open. Obviously his ambition and his religion were in conflict and sometimes he daydreamed about the one way he could fulfill them both. "I should not be surprised," he wrote Laura, "were I to die upon a foreign field, clad in ministerial armor, fighting under the banner of Jesus."

Now Tom worried about Laura. She hadn't been baptized. She didn't eat the proper foods or read the proper books. Romantic novels were what she must have enjoyed for Thomas begged her to give up what he called her "infidel" books. What he feared most was that when Laura died, she wouldn't go to heaven and their family would never be reunited. He wasn't sure that his father would make it, but there was no excuse for Laura. What could she lose by professing her faith? he asked. If there was no after-life, she would be no worse off. But if there was—oh, if there was—she would miss out entirely.

Tom went to see Laura and her family during this period. He worked on Laura's conversion and for a short while he was a hero again, at least within the Arnold family. There was not much enthusiasm for celebrating war heroes now and Thomas Jackson's one day of glory was no longer the "conspicuous" affair it had once been. Moreover, his war experience seemed not to have changed Tom at all. His compulsive habits often made him seem like an old maid; his modest, courtly manners made him appear a kind, old-fashioned gentleman. There was nothing about him to suggest a hero, but he had an admiring family, eager to give him full credit for his exploits.

Certainly to young Tom Arnold (Jackson's namesake and Laura's son), Tom was an honest-to-goodness hero with trophies and souvenirs to prove it. Tom showed the family his Mexican inkstand mounted on doves, his Mexican spurs with their engraved leather straps, his saber, and his Mexican poison spoon. This was a tablespoon with an oblong block of metal inlaid in the bowl which was supposed to change in appearance when touched by poison. Best of all were the gifts—for young Tom, a small brass cannon and a musket with a tin barrel and bayonet.

And of course there were stories and none of them were hard for young Tom to believe. According to him, his uncle proved he was a hero right in Beverly, Virginia, where the Arnolds lived.

One day on a walk, they were approached by a ferocious dog. Young Tom was frightened because he knew just how dangerous the dog was, but his uncle told him to calm down and stay close. Then Thomas Jackson looked that dog right in the eye; he stood still and stared and stared. Pretty soon the dog turned around and slunk off. Well, it was no wonder, young Tom thought, that his uncle had beaten the Mexicans.

That was the last that Thomas Jackson would see of the Arnolds for a long time. He would never see his Uncle Cummins again. The Gold Rush had started and Uncle Cummins, who had accumulated more lawsuits than he could handle, headed west like so many others. But before he'd even had a chance to look for gold, he took sick and died. Tom's childhood was slipping away. He was twenty-six now, facing a future that promised little in the way of fame or excitement.

Then in October, 1850, Tom received orders to go to Fort Meade, Florida. This was Seminole Indian country. Although many of the Seminoles had been transported, those who remained were considered a threat to the settlers. The army's job was to keep peace and Tom was hopeful. Florida was regarded as a frontier; anything might happen there.

🍂🍂 Four

*T*HIRTY *miles from Tampa (the command post*
and nearest point of civilization), Fort
Meade consisted of a group of flimsy
looking buildings surrounded by a maze of rivers
and lakes. To most of the men assigned there, the
sight of such a scraggly, desolate post must have
been discouraging, but not to Lieutenant Jackson
nor to his commanding officer, Captain French.
Both were equally dedicated and ambitious. The
more unpromising a post looked, the greater was
their chance to improve it. The more isolated it
was, the more possibility of danger. In short,
though their salary was meager ($84 a month for
Jackson), both men thought Fort Meade was a
good place to show their abilities. Tom wrote
Laura frankly that his finances did not bother him
in the slightest. All that mattered was a chance to
do something that would make him famous.

Since Jackson and French had been friends in the
Mexican War and since both were hard working,
there was every reason to think they would get
along well. And, indeed, at first they did. As soon

as they had the post in working order, Captain French sent Jackson on a scouting mission to look for Indians on a lake fifty miles northeast of Fort Meade. French was eager for dramatic news to report to headquarters and, of course, Tom was eager to make the news. The trouble was that Tom not only did not see Indians, he traveled ninety miles and couldn't find the right lake. He may have been following inaccurate maps, but Captain French in his report did not give him the benefit of that doubt. Instead he implied that his lieutenant had been incompetent.

Three weeks later (February, 1851) Captain French sent Tom again, this time with instructions to take a different route. Tom found the lake on this trip, but still no Indians. However, he liked scouting very much, he wrote Laura, "but it would be still more desirable if I could have an occasional encounter with Indian parties."

Tom never did have such an encounter. Instead he and Captain French became preoccupied with a building program. Tom was the commissary officer and quartermaster which meant that he was in charge of supplies and equipment of all kinds. And when Tom considered himself in charge, he meant in sole charge. When Captain French, as commanding officer, gave instructions to the builders, Tom resented it, and since the captain wanted to supervise every detail, Tom was out of sorts much of the time. As soon as he gave an order, it seemed, Captain French would come along and

countermand it. Officially the captain had the authority to do this, but Tom found the constant, high-handed use of this authority so humiliating that he convinced himself the captain was overstepping his bounds.

It was obvious that a small, isolated post could not comfortably support two such ambitious, stubborn men, especially when there was no chance, as it turned out, for either of them to become heroes. Both men brooded over their differences with one another. Captain French became more dictatorial, Lieutenant Jackson more stubborn about his rights. They stopped speaking to each other. At last Jackson in desperation wrote the commanding general in Tampa, asking for his support in the matter of authority, but, as Jackson should have realized, the commanding officer had to uphold Captain French's final authority in all matters on the post.

This conflict brought out the worst in both men. Tom's health suffered and his eyes became weak; only his will stiffened. He interpreted the reply of the commanding general as a rebuke, an implication that he did not know the rules. And, of course, if there was anything that Thomas Jackson claimed to know backward and forward, it was rules.

There were, however, all kinds of rules and it soon appeared that Captain French might be breaking rules of another sort. Captain French had been seen walking in the woods with Julie, nursemaid to the Frenchs' children. The enlisted men made jokes about it. So Tom decided that the captain's

behavior should be investigated on moral grounds. He called in the men who had spread the report and he questioned them closely: what had they actually seen? When Captain French heard that his lieutenant was, in effect, spying on him, he charged Jackson with conduct unbecoming a gentleman and an officer and had him put under arrest.

So began a series of charges and countercharges. The post doctor begged Jackson to drop his charges out of kindness to Mrs. French, whom everyone (including Jackson) admired, but Jackson would not do it. Tears came to his eyes at the thought of Mrs. French, but he didn't waver. His Christian duty came first, he said.

The War Department was flooded with mail from Fort Meade, but the general opinion was that two men were making a mountain out of a mole-hill. Jackson was released from arrest and eventually Captain French was transferred to another post under the command of another officer. In the midst of this unpleasant affair, however, Tom was given a chance to take a new turn in his career. He was invited to teach science at the Virginia Military Institute at Lexington, Virginia. He accepted. He knew that as a professor he'd have no chance to win fame, but he would acquire prestige. Moreover, out of courtesy for his honorary rank, he would be called Major Jackson. "I consider the position both conspicuous and desirable," he wrote Laura.

Before assuming his duties in Lexington, Tom went to New York to find a doctor to put him into physical shape for his new job. For six weeks he

was under the care of a Dr. Burney who advised him to relax, to play more, to get married, to drink buttermilk, and to eat cornbread and fruit. He had no trouble following the diet and his health did improve. But Tom had no prospects for marriage and no idea how to relax or how to play. He couldn't even make a small joke without quickly explaining that what he'd said wasn't strictly so. When told that these explanations were not only unnecessary but unattractive, Thomas Jackson replied that he preferred truth to charm.

Certainly the cadets at the Institute did not find him charming or relaxed. They didn't know about his alimentary canal, so when he stood before them at attention, they thought he was trying to impress them with what a good soldier he was. But it was not only his posture that was rigid. Major Jackson seemed unable to bend in any way. He accepted no excuses, overlooked no mistakes, and seldom allowed himself even to smile. Besides, he was boring. He taught the way he learned, as if he were reciting a memorized lesson to a blank wall. If a student said he did not understand a point, Jackson simply repeated what he'd said. He didn't know how to add to an explanation or to clarify it in any other way. In short, he was a poor teacher.

And he was not popular. Old Jack, the cadets called him behind his back, or Tom Fool, or the Iron Duke because of his stiff salute, or Square Box because of his enormous feet. Often he would come into class and find a huge pair of feet drawn on the blackboard. The students wrote notes to each other ("Major T. J. Jackson is as crazy as damnation today") and told stories about the ridiculous lengths he went to observe rules. One very hot spring day, for instance, when both faculty and students had put on summer uniforms, Old Jack appeared, obviously uncomfortable, in his heavy winter uniform. When asked why he hadn't changed, he replied stiffly that he had received no orders to do so. It was impossible for students to imagine Major Jackson playing a heroic role in the Mexican War. Although he was only twenty-seven when he arrived in Lexington, he seemed to them a priggish old man.

Of course Jackson could not help knowing that he was not generally liked by the student body. In 1856 the alumni, aware of the dissatisfaction among the students, made a formal complaint about the mismanagement of his classes. Nothing was done about the complaint, so Jackson may never have fully realized that though he certainly willed to be a good teacher, he was not one. He may have thought that the complaint came as a result of his strictness. If so, this only proved that he was doing his duty, and if he was unpopular, that was nothing to him.

Yet in Lexington society he was generally liked. Thomas Jackson, though he had his own way of doing things, was not a solitary man. He enjoyed company and since it was the fashion in Lexington for people to visit back and forth, Tom visited too. At large parties he was obviously uncomfortable, but there were plenty of young ladies who tried to put him at ease. In smaller groups he learned to relax—in his own way, of course. He made close friends who found the warmth behind his stiff exterior and who appreciated the absolute, childlike sincerity of the man. Tom was unable to pose or pretend to be anything but what he was, yet he was not a simple person. Friends spoke of his humility and his aggressiveness, his severity and his kindliness, and indeed he had all these contradictory traits. They were part of the conflict within him: his ambition at war with his deep determination to be good—in other words, to be selfless.

A few months after arriving in Lexington, he took another step in his religious life. He joined the Presbyterian Church and did it as if he were enlisting in a Supreme Army. He considered his pastor his commanding officer and felt obliged to follow suggestions from the pulpit as if they were official orders. When the pastor remarked that he wished more people would lead the prayer meetings, Tom forced himself to volunteer, though he knew he would sweat as much as if he were before a West Point classroom. When the pastor recommended praying briefly and at frequent intervals, Tom made it a habit to pray whenever he raised a glass of water, sealed an envelope, picked up a letter, and at the end of every class period. Furthermore, he decided to give up dancing and card playing—not that he considered these activities wrong, but he wanted to play safe. "Think and see," he asked Laura whom he was still trying to convert, "if I have ever erred since arriving at mature age." He had, he admitted, told a lie at Chapultepec. He had shouted amid the falling bullets that there was no danger when there obviously was danger. But that was the only lie he'd told in his life and that was before he had officially embraced the Christian religion. So if he couldn't recall a single moral mistake since joining the church, his religion must be a strong one. How could it not also be true? he asked.

Tom took another important step. He got married. Actually, he didn't know that he'd fallen in love until his friend, Major Daniel Hill, told him. Daniel, a classmate of Tom's at West Point, was now on the faculty at Washington College in Lexington, and it was Elinor Junkin, daughter of the president of the college, who aroused in Tom the unusual feeling he couldn't explain. As soon as Tom realized what had happened to him, he was delighted. If he was in love, he would get married. Fortunately, Elinor agreed that it was a good idea, but they kept their plans a secret. Tom never liked to talk about his personal life, so when they were married in August, 1853, they took their friends in Lexington by surprise.

In a way the marriage took Tom by surprise too, for he had never expected to find such happiness in life on earth. He'd always talked to Laura about the happiness they would enjoy in after-life when their family was reunited. But here he was filled to the brim with happiness right *now*. It was as if he were making up for the unhappy years in his childhood when he'd been without a family. Although Ellie (as he called her) adapted to Tom's routines

and accepted his ways, she taught him to unbend and have a good time. And when she told him in the spring of 1854 that they would have a baby, his joy knew no bounds.

The baby was due in October. That summer Tom and Ellie visited Laura, and throughout their travels, Ellie appeared to be in good health. Indeed everything seemed to be going well until the last minute. On October 22 Ellie gave birth to a baby who never lived. What was worse, Ellie, herself, died shortly afterward.

Tom could hardly bear it. For months he went back and forth to her grave site, wishing for his own death so they might be together. Tom's personal life and his religion were so inseparable that he could not help but wonder if he were being punished. Why had it happened? Tom may not have expected to find the answer; yet again, as he had in Mexico, he felt guilty about his ambition. That secret knot was still there. Ellie had known about it. At one point during their brief marriage, Tom had applied for a teaching position at the University of Virginia at Charlottesville. There was an opening in the mathematics department, and although Tom asked influential friends to speak for him, the position was given to someone else. Tom accepted the decision calmly but Ellie had understood his disappointment. A professor at a university outranked one at a military institute and rank still mattered to Tom.

Of course there was no substitute for military fame. Tom never expected to achieve distinction

in that way again, but Ellie must have had a glimpse of his passion for heroism. On their honeymoon they had visited the site in Quebec where one of America's first heroes, General James Wolfe, had been killed. Tom had been moved to the depths of his being. Recalling Wolfe's famous last words, "I die content," Tom responded with the passion of one who envied Wolfe's fate. Of course Wolfe had died content. "To die as he did," Tom asked, "who would not be content?"

Over the years, especially since leaving the army, Tom had tried to channel his ambition into his religion. One was just not consistent with the other. After Ellie's death, he worked on it harder than ever. He made a list in his notebook of his objectives: "To eradicate ambition; to eradicate resentment; to produce humility." It was God's will, not his own, that he tried to accept. Still, one cannot help but suspect that he secretly believed that if he sought God's will with sufficient determination, his own might be fulfilled.

Five

TOM *was so weighed down by his grief that* during his summer vacation in 1856 he went to Europe, hoping to regain an interest in life. He left when the country was in a turmoil over the question of slavery. Should it be legal for settlers in the new western territories to own slaves? People who were in favor of slavery thought it should be legal, that owning slaves was a personal matter—not the business of the national government. People who were against slavery said that slavery was unconstitutional in a country dedicated to the idea that all men were equal. They wanted to get rid of slavery, not to spread it. At the moment these two sides were having a head-on confrontation in the Kansas territory. The matter was supposed to be decided by a vote of the Kansas residents, but instead, guerrilla forces were waging a miniature civil war.

One of the most prominent figures in the fighting was a strange, uneducated, intense, fifty-six-year-old man named John Brown who believed that he had been chosen by God to destroy slavery, by violence if necessary. And in Kansas he believed it was necessary. In retaliation for terrorism on the other side, John Brown and a small band of followers killed five pro-slavery men. He called himself a "special angel of death" and planned to take his war into Virginia when the Kansas campaign was over.

The slavery argument had, of course, been going on for years, erupting like a volcano whenever and wherever the issue became too heated. Thomas Jackson rarely discussed the matter. Too much argument only added to the madness, he said. Although he worried about the consequences of the conflict, he couldn't see that slavery was anything to argue about. God must approve of slavery since there were plenty of slaves in the Bible. And if no one in the Bible questioned the morality of owning slaves, how could he? Still, he did feel concern for black people, just as he had as a boy, and he did feel a responsibility, not only for their physical but for their spiritual well-being. If they became good Christians, he thought, they could at least look forward to happiness in the next world if they didn't find it in this one. So he insisted that his own slaves attend family worship services and he started the first Sunday School for slaves in Lexington.

By the fall of 1856 the disturbances in Kansas had quieted, but the issue of slavery continued to smolder throughout the country. A new political party had been formed which opposed the extension of slavery into the west and challenged the long established Democratic party to which the majority of Southerners belonged. If these new Republicans won the election that fall, the Democrats said, the country would be split apart. The Union would be dissolved. Forty-nine-year-old Abraham Lincoln from Illinois, speaking for the Republicans, said that kind of talk was "humbug." As for John Brown, he of course didn't believe in talk or votes. All he wanted was to continue his war. At the moment he was traveling east, hoping to raise money for guns and ammunition. Considering he was an unschooled man with a life-long record of failures behind him, he did well. Like a fiery prophet from the Old Testament, he spoke with such authority about God's will that he impressed people, even in the most intellectual circles. Obviously John Brown was not only willing to do anything to free the slaves, he was ready, perhaps even eager, to die for the cause. Ralph Waldo Emerson, the famous New England author, called him "the rarest of heroes" and, like many other abolitionists (or anti-slavery people), fell under his spell.

As it turned out, however, it wasn't time for either John Brown or Abraham Lincoln to move to the center of the stage. A Democrat, James Buchanan, won the election of 1856 and Southerners, including Thomas Jackson, generally believed that war had been averted or at least delayed. Jackson had always been a staunch Democrat but he was thinking less about national affairs right now than about personal ones. Refreshed by his trip abroad, he was back in Lexington, ready to start a new life. He'd decided to marry again, and if she would have him, he'd like to marry Mary Anna Morrison, Daniel Hill's sister-in-law, in North Carolina. Tom had made friends with her when she had visited Lexington before he had married Ellie, and although they'd had no contact since, Anna (as he called her) remembered him as fondly as he did her. She was surprised, of course, at his sudden courtship, yet she soon recognized that they were right for each other. Married on July 16, 1857, Tom, at age thirty-three, began another period of profound domestic happiness. He had lived with Ellie's family during his first marriage, but this time he had the added satisfaction of living in a house of his own in Lexington.

As head of what he called his own "establishment," Tom enjoyed being a host and entertaining friends. Of course he'd always lived by routine, but now that he was in command of his own territory, he took special delight in the order around him—everything in place, everything moving according to schedule. There was a time for gardening, a time for study, a time for prayers, a time for conversation. The days moved so smoothly that Tom liked to say he had a house "with golden hinges." Yet for all the order, once he was at home and alone with Anna, Tom was more relaxed than he'd ever been. People who saw him only at church or at work would not have known him at home, Anna claimed. He could be mischievous and playful—jumping out from behind doors to surprise her, grabbing her around the waist to dance the polka.

Still, Tom was frequently not well during these happy years. He complained of his old digestive disorders, of pain in his ears and throat, of neuralgia around his temples. Local doctors could find no cause for any of his troubles, but then no one had ever understood Tom's physical problems. Some of his friends believed that he imagined his illnesses, and indeed a man who worried about the position of his alimentary canal and the weight of his arms must have been overly conscious of his body. He seemed to be at his physical best only when he had to pit himself against dangers or difficulty, so perhaps life was moving too easily on its golden hinges for him to be entirely comfortable.

In February, 1859, Anna gave birth to a baby girl and, of course, he was happier than ever, but when the baby died three months later, Tom asked himself if perhaps he and Anna had not loved the baby too much. Everything belonged to God. Had they thought of the baby as their own? Had Tom put his own will above God's?

In any case, whatever the cause of his ailments, Tom did what he always did when he wasn't well. During vacations he went away to different doctors and sought new remedies. In New York he had part of his tonsils pared away. He visited mineral springs, he rubbed himself with chloroform liniment, he ate brown bread, he sucked lemons, and practiced hydropathy—drinking water and covering himself with cold, wet sheets. The lemons and the sheets worked best, he decided, and in September, 1859, after a treatment at White Sulphur Springs, Virginia, he returned to Lexington, feeling better.

While Tom was lying under wet sheets at White Sulphur Springs, John Brown was less than two hundred miles away, hiding out in a rented farmhouse in the hills across from Harpers Ferry, Virginia. Upstairs in the farmhouse were eighteen men, including two of John Brown's sons. This was the army that Brown had gathered to invade Virginia. Crowded together, they kept quiet and out of sight so as not to arouse the suspicion of neighbors. Downstairs fifteen-year-old Annie Brown stayed on guard so she could alert the household to any danger. John, himself, posing as a cattle buyer named Isaac Smith, waited for more recruits, more money, and for God's signal to start war. With his small army he planned to surprise and capture the Federal arsenal at Harpers Ferry. Beyond that, he was vague about what he would do, confident that when the time came, God would show him. Right now he knew he needed the arms from the arsenal to conduct a war, and when he had those he expected that free black people, slaves, and abolitionists would flock to his side. Together they would march south, freeing slaves as they went. Not all of his army agreed with his scheme. To attack the arsenal was suicidal, some argued, but Brown was determined. "If we lose our lives," he said, "it will perhaps do more for the cause than our lives would be worth in any other way."

On October 15th when three new recruits arrived with $600, John Brown decided that God was ready. The next night the little army, rifles on their shoulders, followed John Brown in his wagon down the dark, winding hills, across a covered bridge, and into the town of Harpers Ferry. The first stages of the operation went surprisingly well. Telegraph wires were cut, two night watchmen were captured, a few hostages on the street were taken. And there was John Brown safe inside the gate of the armory with several million dollars' worth of arms at his disposal. He might have taken the arms then and there and escaped as easily as he had entered, but instead he waited for word to spread and for his new army to gather. Besides, he had one piece of business that he had planned from the beginning. The great-grandnephew of George Washington, Colonel Lewis W. Washington, owned a plantation nearby. If he were taken as a hostage, the whole tone of the raid, Brown thought, would be elevated. Furthermore, Colonel Washington owned a sword that had been the gift of Frederick the Great to Washington. With this sword at his side, John Brown, himself, would feel elevated, as if he were carrying forward the ideals of the American Revolution. Unlike Thomas Jackson who struggled with his heroic notions, John Brown gloried in the idea of himself as a hero.

But even after Colonel Washington had been captured by a detachment of raiders, and even after the famous sword had been strapped around John Brown's waist, no slaves gathered and no volunteers arrived. There was still time to escape, but perhaps John Brown didn't really want to. In any case, while he delayed, the countryside was aroused, militia assembled, and President Buchanan ordered three artillery companies, ninety marines, and Colonel Robert E. Lee to the scene. Thirty-six hours after John Brown had attacked the arsenal, the raid was over. Seventeen lives had been lost (including both of Brown's sons) and John Brown was a prisoner who, if he wasn't lynched or rescued, would certainly be hanged for treason.

Yet Brown had done exactly what he'd set out to do. More than any single individual, he had brought the slavery issue to a head. He had put the south in a panic and given the north a martyr. Moreover, he used the time between his capture and his hanging to create a public image that was hard to resist. Gallant, calm, self-assured, indifferent to his own fate, he did not seem in the courtroom to be an angel of death. He represented himself as a nonviolent man who in his passion to free slaves was only trying to follow the Golden Rule: "Do unto others as you would have them do unto you." He proclaimed his principles in terms that were both reasonable and eloquent. Still, not everyone was impressed. Abraham Lincoln said there was no excuse for what he had done. Some called him an idiot, a madman, a criminal, but the abolitionists up north praised every word he uttered. Emerson went so far as to call Brown a saint and certainly he appeared to die like one. And it was his death, not his life, that was important now.

Thomas Jackson, in charge of a group of cadets who had come to keep peace, was present at the hanging. At the time, of course, no one appreciated the coincidence of these two men being together at this historic moment. Certainly no one would have thought of comparing the two men—one, a rash agitator condemned to death and the other, a shy professor who sucked lemons. Yet for all their major differences, they were in strange ways alike. Both had been deprived of their mothers at the same early age; both were obsessed with obeying the will of God; both were known for strictness with subordinates, frustration under command, and though no one would have suspected either of heroism, both would be hailed as heroes capable of extraordinary performance under the pressure of their times. Each, one a law-defying loner and one a law-respecting military officer, would come to be regarded as a symbol of his cause.

Tom's interest in Brown at the moment was in the way he met death. Indeed Tom seemed to be fascinated by every detail of the spectacle. He noticed that Brown wore white socks, that his slippers were "predominately red," that the coffin, upon which he sat on the way to the gallows, was made of black walnut. John Brown behaved, Tom said, "with unflinching firmness" and "ascended the scaffold with apparent cheerfulness." Yet at the last minute Tom was so awed by the thought of a man who must surely be standing at the very brink of hell that he found himself praying for Brown's soul. He doubted that it would do much good since Brown had been offered the services of a minister but had refused. (Tom may or may not have known that Brown had scoffed at the value of prayers that a southern minister might offer.) In any case, on December 2, 1859, John Brown died on the gallows and Thomas Jackson returned to Lexington with solemn thoughts and a head cold.

There was talk of war now on all sides. Was Brown's raid part of a northern conspiracy? Papers had been found in Brown's hideout indicating that prominent abolitionists had given him money. Would there be more raids, more violence? Could anyone in the south feel safe?

"I think we have great reason for alarm," Thomas Jackson wrote, "but my trust is in God."

❧❧❧ Six

*T*HE *next year, 1860, was an election year and politicians on both sides played upon the fears of the people.* At first Tom was optimistic. He was "pretty well satisfied," he said, "that the Northern people love the Union more than they do their peculiar notions of slavery." But when the Democrats, unable to agree on their principles, split into three separate parties and when the Republicans nominated Abraham Lincoln for president, Tom was less confident. Lincoln made it clear that although he would not meddle with slavery in the south, he was absolutely opposed to the extension of slavery into the west. Most southerners considered that this interference was unconstitutional. The national government was not only taking over powers that belonged to the states, they said, it was favoring the interests of the north over the south. From the earliest days of the nation, the north and the south had contended for power and now that the west was opening up, it was almost inevitable that the struggle would be extended. The only solution, some southerners argued, was for southern states to secede from the Union and form a separate nation of their own. They hoped they wouldn't need to fight for their independence, but if they had to they would.

Moderate men in both the north and the south worked desperately all year for some kind of compromise that would insure peace. Thirty-six-year-old Thomas Jackson was one of the moderates. He intended to support the Union, but if Virginia was invaded would he transfer his loyalty to the south? His state would come first. Meanwhile he believed that the less said about the conflict, the better.

He went about his normal business: planting lettuce, teaching classes, and as summer approached, he and Anna made arrangements to go to Vermont to try a new water cure. But when Lincoln was elected in the fall, there was no use pretending that life would or could go on as usual. South Carolina seceded from the Union on December 20, 1860, and Jackson believed that only God could avert war now. If Christians all over the country could unite on one special day and pray for peace, Tom thought, God might yet come to the rescue. But if He didn't, there was nothing more that anyone could do.

Throughout the nation peace-loving people had the same idea and agreed to set January 4th aside as a day for prayer. Unfortunately, however, nothing stopped the course of events already in motion. On January 9th Mississippi seceded from the Union and within the next three weeks five more states (though not Virginia) had joined the ranks. Two weeks later the seceding states (or Confederacy) had formed a government and had elected a Mississippi senator, Jefferson Davis, as president.

The immediate point of danger that spring was Fort Sumter, South Carolina, where in spite of secession, federal troops were still stationed and the Union flag still flew. The issue was coming to a head because the men at Fort Sumter were running out of food. This was the dilemma: if Lincoln withdrew the men, as South Carolina requested, he would be abandoning a federal fortress, but if he sent in provisions, he might be starting a war. In effect, he would be saying that he didn't recognize secession, that the fort was Union property, and that he intended to protect and sustain it. As for the Confederacy, it could not permit the Union, which had become a foreign nation, to maintain a fort within its borders.

On April 6th Lincoln notified the governor of South Carolina that he planned to send provisions to Fort Sumter. On Friday, April 12th, the newly formed Confederate army opened fire on the fort and within two days had demolished it.

By April 13th the news of the firing on Fort Sumter had spread through much of the south. Certainly it had reached Lexington and excited the cadets. Since this was a Saturday, many of them were already in town, looking for a bit of fun. In the general spirit of celebration, a group of cadets tore down the Union flag and ran up the Virginia flag in its place. Arguments followed, turned into fights, and then into a general free-for-all. In the end all the disorderly cadets were rounded up and herded into a large classroom where officers tried to calm them down with talk about military discipline. Still, the cadets were restless.

Then Thomas Jackson entered the room. The cadets laughed and called for Old Jack. The strictest officer of them all, a prim letter-of-the-law man who pounced on the slightest infringement of the most piddling rule, what would he say to this large-scale outbreak?

Thomas Jackson stepped up to the platform. For a moment he looked the cadets over as if he were measuring them not according to classroom standards but according to a grim reality beyond their experience. Then his eyes took fire and he spoke with a passion that both dazzled and sobered the young men. This was a side of Old Jack that no one had ever suspected.

"The time for war has not yet come," he said, "but it will come, and that soon; and when it does come, my advice is to draw the sword and throw away the scabbard."

Old army feelings were obviously stirring in Thomas Jackson as he spoke, yet he had not allowed himself to respond to this war as he had to the Mexican War or indeed as he might have to any foreign war. The enemy was not foreign this time but people he knew—fellow cadets at West Point like George McClellan of Pennsylvania and Ambrose Burnside, childhood playmates like Joe Lightburn, and veterans of the Mexican War like

General Winfield Scott who had once praised him so highly, and even members of his own family. Ellie's father, who had remained one of Tom's closest friends, was a staunch Union man. Laura, who had recently made Thomas so happy by accepting the Christian faith, would be on the enemy's side, for she and her family had always opposed slavery.

The break came just four days after the flagpole incident. Virginians decided to secede when President Lincoln called for 75,000 volunteers to put down insurrection. This was tantamount to invasion, Virginians declared. It was war. There was no room now for sentiment. Thomas Jackson flung himself single-mindedly into the business he knew best. But if the cadets expected to see Old Jack replaced by the fiery commander they had glimpsed the other night, they would be disappointed. On April 21st, Jackson was ordered to march the cadets to Richmond, leaving Lexington at 12:30 P.M. In ranks ahead of the appointed time, the cadets were impatient to go but Jackson would not give the order. When asked why they couldn't leave, Jackson pointed to the clock on the Institute steeple. It was not 12:30 yet and they would not march until the minute hand had reached the exact spot it was supposed to. The cadets exchanged glances. The same Old Jack they'd known in class was in charge again.

Actually, the same Old Jack—stern, demanding, inflexible—was exactly what the army needed at the moment. Too many people in both the north and south were looking upon the war as a grand outing. Young men who had expected to spend their lives on a farm, in a factory or an office acted as if they had suddenly been let out of school. Kissing their girls good-bye, shouldering their rifles, they marched away like storybook heroes while bands played and flags flew. They'd be back soon, they shouted, for hadn't the newspapers promised them a short war? Those in high command, of course, might not be so optimistic but the majority of untrained soldiers, both Yankees and Rebels (as they came to be called), believed in a quick, easy victory for their side. One big battle and it might be all over.

Nowhere were Confederate soldiers having a better time than they were in Harpers Ferry, Virginia. When the Union army had decided the city was indefensible and had moved out, the Virginia militia had moved in, whooping like boys on a picnic. What's more, they had been whooping ever since. On April 23rd Thomas Jackson, now a colonel, arrived to take charge. The first thing he did was to order every liquor barrel in town rolled out in the streets and emptied into the gutters. Then after recruiting men from the militia (a temporary state unit) into the regular army, he began to show what he meant by military discipline. In the first place, the discipline applied to everyone. Young aristocratic gentlemen, unaccustomed to dirty jobs, had to empty garbage and clean toilets, the same as everyone else. In the second place, discipline meant long hours, beginning at five in the morning and often not ending until ten at night. There was machinery to be made; defenses to be established, arms and food to be secured. There was target practice, guard duty, and most important—drilling and more drilling. If there weren't enough guns to go around, those without guns had to go through the motions of the drill anyway.

Old Jackson was a hard man, the soldiers said. And a queer one. He never seemed to sleep, spoke only when spoken to, and sucked lemons constantly. It was said that every Sunday morning before going to church he lay under cold, wet sheets to improve his digestion. There was no doubt that Jackson had established order in Harpers Ferry, but with all his petty rules and regulations, he didn't seem like a man for the battlefield. Not like Colonel "Jeb" Stuart, for instance, who was the very picture of a dashing hero with his golden spurs, his plumed hat, and his scarlet-lined coat. Nor like the dignified and handsome General Robert E. Lee who seemed to have been born for his role.

Colonel Jackson, with his wrinkled, old Institute cap pulled down over his nose, looked more like a farmer than an officer, and not even his horse improved his image. Although Jackson had several imposing horses at his disposal, his favorite was Little Sorrel, a short, sturdy workhorselike animal that he had bought from a carload of captured Union horses and intended for his wife. In the end he had kept the horse for himself, for Little Sorrel turned out to be tough and tireless, with an easy, rocking gait that suited Jackson perfectly. But military? Soldiers grinned at the sight of the awkward officer and his undersized horse. They were a pair, those two.

In the middle of May, Jackson, who had been given a brigade of Virginia mountain men, began conducting a series of reconnaissance marches. His men, obviously still in love with the idea of war, were thrilled to be acting like real soldiers. In June one young man wrote: "Marching went quite hard with us, especially myself, who had never marched a day in my life." Yet at the end of the day after a "good wash" and refreshments, he was happy to report that all the men "felt like soldiers indeed, with our clothes covered with brass buttons, and the ladies smiling at us out of the corners of their mouths." He couldn't get over the glory of it all. Five days later he was describing another march and more ladies who waved their handkerchiefs as the men passed. "Oh! how nice to be a soldier," he sighed.

The first time that Jackson's men actually came into contact with the Union army (July 2nd), they were so fascinated, they broke ranks and climbed fences for a better view. All those mounted men! The bands! The flying colors! Overcome by the spectacle, the men forgot for a moment that this was the enemy; they were to be fought, not admired. Jackson quickly set them straight. He had no hope of defeating the enemy since there were so many of them, but he had no intention of letting them get away easily either. He had his men charge when they could, and when they couldn't, he led

them slowly back, fighting every inch of the way. Eventually Jackson's brigade made it safely back to the main army and the Union forces gave up the chase. The encounter had not been heated enough to show Jackson at his blazing best, but his men were impressed. The old Lemon-Squeezer was a first-class fighter, after all, they admitted. In turn, Jackson was proud of his brigade.

By now northerners and southerners alike were restless for the real war to begin. The northern press was particularly aggressive. Let the fighting start! Get it over! Take Richmond, the Confederate capital! Soldiers and citizens took up the cry—"On to Richmond!" It sounded so sure and gay and easy, but General Irvin McDowell, who was supposed to get the Union troops to Richmond, did not think it would be easy at all. There hadn't been time enough to train his army, he said. They were inexperienced. President Lincoln pointed out that the Confederate army was inexperienced too. And the decision was made: On to Richmond as soon as possible!

On July 16th General McDowell and 30,000 soldiers started their march, knowing that at Manassas, only thirty miles from Washington, a Confederate army waited with General Johnson (in command of the Army of Northern Virginia) and with General Beauregard who had ordered the first gun to be fired at Fort Sumter. A second Union army was patrolling the hills west of Manassas to keep Confederate reinforcements away from the battle—specifically, the Army of the Shenandoah of which Jackson and his brigade were a part.

As the participants gathered at Manassas, excitement mounted. At last! This was it! The war was starting! Victory was in the air as if nothing else could possibly exist. The Confederates, obviously outnumbered, were lined up in a defensive position beside a small stream known as Bull Run, but if they worried, they didn't show it. Hadn't they always believed that one rebel could beat five Yankees? As for the Yankees, they straggled down to Manassas, stopping to pick blackberries—in no hurry, for hadn't they been told that the Rebs would run once they saw how bold the Yanks were? Even the civilians in Washington, high-ranking officials and their wives, were so sure of a Union victory that they planned to picnic on the outskirts of Manassas on the Big Day. They would drink champagne and toast the army and cry "Bravo! Bravo!" What could be nicer?

Although there had been several days of initial skirmishing, the Big Day turned out to be Sunday, July 21st. A beautiful sunny day—perfect for a picnic. Carriages were drawn up on a hill overlooking Bull Run; ladies rustled under parasols; gentlemen adjusted field glasses; couriers galloped up with the latest news. Good news, all of it. Yankee advances. Confederate confusion. So it went for the first six hours.

Yet not all the Confederates had been heard from. The Army of the Shenandoah that was supposed to be held in the hills by the Union watchdog forces had eluded their enemy on July 18th and had

71

left for Manassas. At first they'd been slow. The men didn't know where they were going or why and saw no reason to rush just because their officers told them to. Finally Jackson, whose brigade led the march, stopped them and read an official statement. "Our gallant army under General Beauregard is now attacked by overwhelming numbers," Jackson read. He asked the troops if they would not "step out like men and make a forced march to save the country."

A battle! The men yelled their approval—a special rebel yell. Half Indian war whoop, half wolf howl with maybe a touch of wildcat in it, it was a fierce sound that a Yankee soldier once said sent a corkscrew sensation down the spine. Woh-who-ey. The yell rose to a pitch on the *who* and held there, trembling and drawn out, then fell with a thud on the *ey*. The men quickened their pace. Woh-who-ey. For eighteen hours they marched until at last, having waded waist deep through the green Shenandoah River, they dropped, exhausted. They marched and they rode a train for a few hours, and then they marched again. But they were there now. The question was: Were they in time?

By noon on the 21st it was clear that Beauregard had positioned the major part of his army in the wrong place. While the enemy was concentrating its forces on the left, the Confederates were wasting their time on the right. In the general scramble to change positions, Jackson and his brigade found themselves in the thick of the activity. Union men were in the distance but steadily advancing; the Confederates were retreating. As one officer passed Jackson, he shook his head. "The day is going against us," he said.

"If you think so, sir," Jackson replied, "don't say anything about it."

Jackson did not plunge forward to meet the enemy, as his men might have expected. Looking over the field, he saw a plateau which he recognized as the best possible position for making a stand. Here he placed his men and artillery and when the enemy fire closed in, Jackson stood before his brigade, his blue eyes blazing, the old battle fever upon him. Walking back and forth, indifferent to bullets, he was lifted out of himself, possessed with a power he'd known only once before, in Mexico. He understood exactly how to get the most out of every man and every gun and he *willed* victory into the day. "The fight," as one officer put it, "was just then hot enough to make [Jackson] feel well." Shot in the hand as he held it up, Jackson wrapped a handkerchief around the wound and went on as if nothing had happened.

In another part of the field, General Bee, a West Point classmate of Jackson's, was desperately trying to stop a retreat. "Look yonder!" he cried to his men. "There's Jackson standing like a stone wall."

General Bee was killed almost as soon as he'd finished speaking, but retreating Confederates did see how well Jackson's line was holding and gradually they began to rally around it. The last reinforcements from Shenandoah army, which had just arrived, were rushed to the scene. And the tide of the battle began to turn.

When the center of the Union line was in plain sight, General Beauregard ordered a charge. Jackson relayed the order.

"Reserve your fire till they come within fifty yards," he shouted, "then fire and give them the bayonet. And when you charge, yell like furies."

The orders were carried out precisely.

Woh-who-ey!

Woh-who-ey!

Suddenly the entire Union army was falling back, then turning around and hurrying off the field. A huge, confused mob mixed with panic-stricken picnickers headed pell-mell back to Washington.

The battle was over and with it some of the innocent glory was gone. For the fields were strewn with bodies—young men who only the day before had been laughing and making jokes. Two thousand Confederates killed or wounded; three thousand Union men. Stopped right in the midst of doing something. In the middle of a sentence perhaps, in mid-step, in the act of raising a rifle, at the beginning of a smile. Struck down, blown apart as if they weren't *people*. As if they weren't *young*. How could inexperienced men have imagined what death would be like on a battlefield?

In one day soldiers on both sides became veterans, but of course the victors felt better than the losers. If they could win a battle, southerners said, they could win a war.

Thomas Jackson wrote Anna about his part in the fighting: "God made my brigade more instrumental than any other," he said, "in repulsing the main attack."

For once Jackson did not try to disguise his pride or his ambition. A few weeks before he had been made a brigadier general. He'd had all he "ought to desire in the way of a promotion," he wrote Anna, but it was clear that what he ought to desire was not necessarily what he did desire. Yet he could hardly have expected his desires to be fulfilled so soon. Within three months he was pushed up another step and made a major general. This time he could not allow either himself or Anna to take pride in his achievement. "I trust my darling little wife," he wrote, "feels more gratitude to our kind Heavenly Father than pride or elation at my promotion." It was as if he had been so favored, he had to be careful to give God all the credit lest the favors stop.

But Tom was not only a major general; he had earned another name. The newspapers had picked up General Bee's remark on the battlefield at Manassas and from now on Tom would be known as General Stonewall Jackson. Or more often, just plain Stonewall. If he wanted to be "noticed," General Bee had done him a favor. People couldn't help noticing a man called Stonewall.

✿✿ Seven

AS Tom was called *Stonewall, so his brigade,*
officially the First Brigade, became known
as the Stonewall Brigade. The men took
pride in the name for they had come not only to
admire the Old Man, as they sometimes called him,
but to feel affection for him. Stonewall couldn't
ride past them now without being cheered. Of
course, they admitted, he didn't look like much.
Soldiers who had never seen him shook their heads
in disbelief. "*That's* Stonewall Jackson?" they would
ask and the men in his brigade would grin with
pleasure. Yes, they would brag, that plain man sitting on that plain little horse sucking a lemon—that
was Stonewall Jackson. The one and only. Yes, he
sucked lemons much of the time. And yes, he had
other peculiarities. The men took endless delight
in talking about them.

"You notice he never puts pepper on his food?"

"Why's that?"

"He believes that pepper made his left leg weaker
than his right."

"You know what he's doing half the time he's riding Little Sorrel?"

"What?"

"Praying."

"With his eyes open?"

"Yep. He looked all through the Bible to see if there's a rule about a person having to close his eyes to pray. He couldn't find any so he figures it's all right to pray any time he takes the notion, eyes open or not."

On October 21st the news came that Stonewall and his brigade would be separated. All fall changes had been taking place in the armies on both sides. President Lincoln, after the disaster at Manassas, had taken the command of the Union army away from General McDowell and given it to General George McClellan, or "Little Mac," as his men called him. McClellan was popular, cautious, and thorough. And he was not going to risk another encounter with the enemy until he thought his army was ready for it. While he embarked on a strict program of training, other Union forces moved into northwestern Virginia, just above the Shenandoah Valley. Of course the Valley people became nervous. "Send us back General Jackson," they begged the War Department. So Thomas Jackson was given an independent command in charge of the defense of the Valley district. His brigade, however, would be left behind.

Before leaving for Winchester, his new head-quarters, Tom called the brigade together to say good-bye. They came—five regiments, about 5,000 men—and stood at attention while Stonewall rode before them on Little Sorrel. Sitting erect in his saddle, Stonewall looked at his beloved brigade which he had trained, marched, fought with for seven difficult months. He said all the proper words of praise and encouragement that a commanding officer would be expected to say. Then as if he suddenly felt this was not enough, he stood up in his stirrups, his eyes blazing, and cried out to his men:

"In the Army of the Shenandoah you were the First Brigade; in the Army of the Potomac you were the First Brigade; in the second corps of this army you are the First Brigade; you are the First Brigade in the affections of your General; and I hope by your future deeds and bearings you will be handed down to posterity as the First Brigade in our second War of Independence. Farewell!"

As Stonewall turned aside, the brigade broke out in a deafening cheer that filled the morning, echoed, and followed him off the field. But as it turned out, the War Department changed its mind. The next day orders came that Stonewall could have his brigade, after all. Of course in his new position Stonewall would not be in direct command of the brigade, which was assigned to General Richard Garnett. But the men liked General Garnett and at least they'd be fighting with Stonewall and cheering him when he passed, just as they always had. And they'd be hearing all the Stonewall stories. Indeed, they had hardly settled down in Winchester when the persimmon tree story went the rounds.

It seemed that on a recent expedition the Old Man had noticed a tree full of ripe, red persimmons. Now, there was nothing he enjoyed more than a good persimmon, so he jumped down from his horse, climbed the tree, and before anyone realized what he was doing—there he was, sitting among the branches, stuffing himself with ripe, red persimmons. But when he started to come down, he couldn't. He'd maneuvered himself into a position where he could move neither up nor down. He was stuck.

So what happened?

Well, much as he hated to, he called for help and his staff rigged up a ramp out of fence rails for him to climb down on. The general was not overly amused.

Stories like this could have kept the army at Winchester entertained all winter, but Stonewall was not interested in entertaining anyone. Already disappointed that he hadn't been allowed to pursue the retreating Yankees after Manassas, he was determined now to attack, capture, disrupt, or disperse enemy detachments, some of which lay no more than fifty miles from Winchester. So while the army was still enjoying what it considered its Christmas vacation, it received orders to march.

On New Year's Day, 1862, the men started out, not knowing, of course, that what Stonewall Jackson had in mind was a 150-mile, triangle-shaped march through mountains that could, and often did, become all but impassable in January. There were three enemy posts that Stonewall hoped to wipe out, but it was the weather and not the Yankees that turned out to be the real enemy. Before the first day was over, the men were battling a fierce sleet storm. Sharp fingernails of ice stabbed their faces, bottled up trees, glazed the roads. The supply wagons fell so far behind that the men had neither food nor blankets that night. Nor the next. On the third day General Garnett halted his brigade on the roadside to cook whatever rations they had been able to scrape together or secure from the rear.

In the midst of this makeshift meal General Jackson rode up. What was the meaning of the recess? he asked.

General Garnett explained that it was impossible for the men to walk farther without eating.

"Impossible" was a word that infuriated Thomas Jackson. "I have never found anything impossible with this brigade," he snapped.

He was the Lexington professor again, laying down rules, rejecting excuses. Private property was not to be molested on this march, he announced. Fences were not to be used for campfires, no matter how cold it might be. When a captain pulled up the fences on his own property which the army happened to be passing, Jackson suspended him from duty.

Yet Stonewall Jackson shared the men's hardships, sleeping under trees, helping to push artillery and wagons up slippery mountain roads, pulling fallen horses to their feet, showing concern for boys who were hurt. So when they could find breath enough, the men cheered him as usual, but they grumbled too. Old Fool Jackson, they muttered. He'd do anything to chase Yankees.

"I just wish all the Yankees would go to hell," one footsore soldier moaned.

"Well," a comrade replied, "Old Stonewall would only follow them there. And drag us with him."

The expedition lasted twenty-four days and when it was over a lieutenant wrote to his mother. "Ma," he said, "the romance of the thing is entirely worn off, not only with myself but with the whole army."

Stonewall, however, returning to Winchester where Anna was spending the winter, was entirely satisfied. He had scared the enemy away from two posts (Bath and Romney) and he had freed three counties that had been under their control.

Jackson's army had just two months of camp life before spring came, pushing violets up through the ground, splashing blossoms over cherry trees. But spring was hard to bear this year. All those lilac bushes sweetening up the soft air! A person could not help but ask: How many men would be around to take joy in the next springtime? Yet there was no stopping the war. It was knit so tightly into the calendar that one went ahead with the other. By the middle of March George McClellan was preparing for his attack on Richmond. He wouldn't march his army south as McDowell had done; he'd go by water—sail down the Potomac River below Richmond and then march back. But President Lincoln couldn't leave Washington undefended and he worried about Stonewall Jackson, only seventy miles away, in Winchester. So he sent General Banks and General Shields with 23,000 men into the Shenandoah Valley to take care of Stonewall.

Everyone was on the move. While Banks and Shields marched toward Winchester, Stonewall's smaller army moved south. The Yankees followed. Each army had its scouts out to determine what the other army was doing but the information that came back was in both cases inaccurate. The Union generals were told they had chased Jackson far enough away so that he was no longer a threat. So Banks decided to go to the support of McClellan and let Shields and his 9,000 men stay in the valley. Jackson heard about the move and made plans to attack Shields. His job was to keep as many Union forces away from McClellan as possible. If he was successful against Shields (and he expected to be) he might bring Banks back to the valley. But Jackson was figuring that he had more men than Shields when in fact he had only half as many.

On March 22nd Jackson ordered a forced march. Although there were many stragglers, most of the men managed to cover between twenty and twenty-seven miles the first day. On the second day they marched fourteen miles in the morning; in the afternoon they met the enemy at the village of Kernstown. Jackson placed Garnett and the Stonewall Brigade at the center of action, then went to the top of a nearby hill where he could observe the full scope of the battle and direct accordingly.

At first Jackson was pleased. His old brigade was facing heavy fire but they were advancing. Then something seemed to go wrong. The fire from the enemy was becoming more and more intense and suddenly the Confederates were retiring. Jackson could see now that there were far more Union men than he had anticipated. But withdraw? Without a specific order from him?

Furious, he galloped down the hill, stopped a retreating private, and asked him just where he thought he was going.

"To the rear, sir," the private stammered. "I've run out of cartridges."

"Then go back and give them the bayonet," Stonewall thundered as he charged on to the field. He expected to confront his old brigade, inspire them as he always had, and lead them back to battle. But it was too late. Out of ammunition, the brigade was in full retreat under the orders of General Garnett. Stonewall Jackson grabbed a drummer boy. He held his shoulder in an iron grip. "Beat the rally," he commanded. "Beat it."

The frightened drummer boy beat, but General Garnett had decided that it was suicidal to fight such superior forces without ammunition. He had already formed a line in the rear to cover the retreat and save the wagons and artillery. Stonewall could do nothing more.

The battle at Kernstown had lasted just three hours but it had seemed endless. That evening a private in the horse battery wrote home: "Mother, Home, Heaven are all sweet words, but the grand-

est sentence I ever heard . . . was, 'Boys, the battle is over.' "

Defeated or not, Stonewall would have the satisfaction of knowing that his action had given the Union leaders second thoughts. General Banks returned to the valley and President Lincoln ordered General McDowell to remain close enough to Washington to defend it, if necessary.

But Stonewall did not like to be defeated and he took steps to see that it wouldn't happen again. The first thing he did was to reorganize the cavalry which was responsible for supplying him with information about the enemy. Then he worked out a marching schedule which was intended to eliminate straggling. The army would rest ten minutes out of every hour—not just lounge around but lie down flat on their backs. Stonewall believed a person rested best if he rested all over. (When the program was put in practice, Little Sorrel of his own accord lay down with the men.)

Then Stonewall studied the maps of the valley until he was familiar with every mountain pass, every back road, and, as some said, every cow path and goat track. He was going to bottle those Union soldiers up in the valley by keeping them on the jump. He would spring out when least expected. He would mystify everyone. He wouldn't even tell his own officers what his strategy was. Indeed, he'd be as secretive as Frederick the Great who said if he thought his own coat knew his plans, he'd take it off and burn it.

Stonewall made another change. A week after

the battle, he removed General Garnett from his command and placed him under arrest, charging him with giving an unauthorized order and disrupting a battle. The camp went into an uproar. The unanimous reaction was that Stonewall was being unfair; he couldn't stand defeat and resented any decisions but his own. Those who had fought with Garnett believed that, if anything, he'd waited too long to order withdrawal. The Stonewall Brigade was outraged. For three weeks they let General Jackson come and go without raising a single cheer, not even looking at him if they could help it. Yet no matter what anyone said, Stonewall would not withdraw his charges against Garnett any more than he'd been willing to withdraw his charges against Captain French in Florida. Some of his fellow officers said Stonewall had a cruel streak in him, but perhaps being so harsh in performing what he called his duty gave Stonewall a sense of righteousness when things were going against him. Perhaps it was his way of putting himself on God's side at a time when God did not appear to be conspicuously on his. Stonewall was certainly thinking about God, worrying about the fact that he had fought the battle of Kernstown on Sunday in spite of his belief that Sunday should be devoted to the worship of God. He made it a rule not even to write a letter on Sunday or read one if it was delivered to him. He hadn't wanted to fight, he told Anna, but there had been no way out of it. So how could he have been wrong? How could he blame himself?

In any case, the war went on as wars do, tearing at men's nerves, exposing the best and worst in them. General Garnett, although not returned to his old brigade, was released from arrest by the War Department. And Stonewall Jackson began his campaign in which he meant to surprise and mystify everyone.

The Shenandoah Valley was scattered with nests of enemy forces—General Banks, General Shields, General Milroy, General Fremont, and at Fredericksburg General McDowell, close enough to be called at any time. Against all this opposition, Jackson was finally given some help. General Richard ("Old Baldy") Ewell and 7,000 men came swinging up the eastern side of the valley at the end of April. Four abreast they marched, singing:

Listen to the mockingbird,
Listen to the mockingbird,
The mockingbird, still singing o'er the
grave . . .

They camped near Culpeper while General Ewell waited for orders. But Stonewall, busy working out his secret moves, was not ready to send orders. As Ewell waited, he picked up bits and pieces of contradictory news and became more and more impatient. He couldn't bear uncertainty; it gave him indigestion. In the best of times he could eat only one food, a special kind of wheat cereal, and even that was not agreeing with him now. General Ewell fussed and fumed; he had never, he said, felt worse in his life.

The troops who served directly under Stonewall were equally as confused and frustrated. On April 30, 1862, Stonewall sent the cavalry in one direction and the infantry and the artillery in another. The enemy decided that Jackson was leaving the valley, probably going to Richmond. Jackson's own troops thought so too, but they couldn't see why, when there were good roads available, Jackson had to march them down a rough, muddy back road that ran beside the river. The quartermaster, struggling to move his wagons through the muck, summed up the general feeling. "Jackson," he said, "is a cracked man."

On the third day, however, instead of continuing south toward Richmond, the army was put on a train and sent back west to Staunton, an area that General Milroy was threatening. On May 8th Jackson's army met Milroy's at the little town of McDowell, twenty-five miles west of Staunton. They fought a hard, five-hour battle in which the Confederates lost 498 men and the Union army lost 256. It was not a defeat or victory for either side, but it wasn't over either. Jackson's men expected the battle to continue the next day. The following morning they found, however, that Milroy's army had crept away in the middle of the night, leaving their campfires burning. If the enemy had withdrawn, Jackson figured, the Confederates had won. He sent General Ewell a straightforward announcement: "Yesterday God gave us the victory at McDowell."

Stonewall's next target was General Banks, although of course no one knew this, Banks least of all. Banks had arranged his army in a triangle at the center of the valley: part in Front Royal, part in Winchester, and part in Strasburg, his own headquarters. But at the moment Banks wasn't worried about a thing. The Union forces had just taken New Orleans, been victorious at Mississippi, and were threatening Richmond. General Shields, Fremont, and Milroy had all moved out of the area. General Banks not only did not expect trouble, he complained of life being dull. He just didn't have the kind of mind that could imagine rapid marches and tricky maneuvers going on behind his back. He had been informed that Stonewall Jackson was in Harrisonburg, several days' march to the south, and as far as he was concerned, that's where Jackson stayed.

In actual fact Jackson had at last joined up with Ewell and together they were proceeding toward Front Royal. Not directly, of course. He took his infantry on such a roundabout route that General Taylor, a Louisianian with Ewell, accused Jackson of giving them a scenic tour. But at one o'clock on the afternoon of May 23rd, Stonewall Jackson's army reached the outskirts of Front Royal. They were met by a nineteen-year-old girl dressed in white, running and waving her bonnet. This was Belle Boyd, a Confederate spy.

"I knew it was Stonewall when I heard the guns," she said. "Tell him to charge right down and he will catch them all."

It didn't turn out to be quite as easy to do as

Belle made it sound, but Jackson did catch them—if not all, nearly all.

Now for the next move. Jackson figured that as soon as Banks heard about Front Royal, he would move toward Winchester, and Jackson hoped to confront him on the way. So he ordered his men to go to bed and be up "at earliest dawn," as he always said, ready to march. Meanwhile in Strasburg, Banks refused to be alarmed by the Front Royal news. It must be a small raiding party poking about, he said. It couldn't be Stonewall Jackson; he was in Harrisonburg. It wasn't until eight hours later when someone reported actually seeing Stonewall at Front Royal that General Banks decided to move.

The turnpike to Winchester was a busy place the next day. From dawn the Confederates marched, fighting enemy units on the way, cavalry charging against cavalry, infantry detouring around thrashing horses and dying men but going relentlessly on, one foot after another, through the morning, the afternoon, the evening, and into the night. They couldn't stop; by daylight they must have their artillery in the Winchester hills, Jackson said. Some men closed their eyes and walked in a semi-conscious state; some fell, simply unable to take the next step. At two in the morning Jackson gave the men two hours sleep; they dropped in their tracks but were up again at four, knowing that at the end of all their weary walking, there was still a battle to be fought.

The Yankees were in the hills when Jackson's

army reached Winchester but they had not yet managed to move their artillery in place. Still, the hill had to be taken, batteries had to be wiped out, Union troops massed on lower ridges had to be driven away.

By seven-thirty in the morning it was over. Jackson's men had accomplished what Jackson had expected of them. General Taylor led the final charge up the hill and as Union troops fled, Stonewall Jackson took off his old cap and waved it wildly in the air.

"Very good!" he shouted. "Now let's holler!"

Woh-who-ey!

Woh-who-ey!

Afterward General Taylor said that what he remembered most vividly about the battle was a bluebird flying right through the gunfire with a worm in its mouth. Stubborn and bold as the Old Man himself.

Jackson was back in the good graces of his brigade now and as popular as ever. He was hard; everyone agreed to that. They all remembered the story about the young soldier who on Jackson's orders had been shot twenty minutes after he'd broken into a private home and insulted the ladies there. But every general occasionally took extreme measures to enforce discipline. It took a hard man to win a war, didn't it? And for all his shenanigans on back roads, he had proved he knew what he was doing. The men might grumble about him, but generally they ended up shrugging their shoulders. That was just Stonewall's way, they said.

Sometimes they liked Stonewall's way; sometimes they didn't. They liked the fact that he didn't put on airs, that he ate with his men, that he was just as polite to the humblest private as to the bigwigs. They did wish, however, that he would recognize that some things were not possible for some men. He classed "all who were weak and weary, who fainted by the wayside," one soldier said, "as men wanting in patriotism." Some knew about the officer who had been refused a furlough when his wife was dying. The army wasn't giving furloughs, Jackson had snapped. Didn't he love his country more than his wife? The officer never forgave Jackson.

In general, however, the men understood Stonewall now; he was a "one-idea-ed man" intent on victory, and if they had to fight, they preferred fighting with him than with anyone else. So when the citizens of Winchester, celebrating the return of the Confederates, declared that Stonewall Jackson was the Champion of the Valley, the old brigade cheered until they were hoarse. Stonewall was *theirs*, they pointed out.

🌰🌰 Eight

WHEN *General Banks marched out of Winchester*, he didn't stop until he'd crossed the Potomac River and was safe again on northern soil.

"We have 'busted' Banks," Jackson's quartermaster gloated, hoping that at last the army could settle down for a well-earned rest. But President Lincoln could not let Stonewall Jackson rest for fear he'd move toward Washington. So he ordered General Fremont to return to the Valley with 17,000 men and he ordered General McDowell, who was on his way to Richmond, to send 20,000 men to the Valley. (McDowell assigned General Shields and his army to the job.) Coming from different directions, the two Union generals planned to catch Stonewall's army (about 15,000) neatly between them. Actually, when the Union officers communicated with each other, they spoke of "bagging" Jackson as if he were a fox that they would run down. But Stonewall Jackson was a slyer fox than any of his hunters imagined. He knew if he were quick enough, he could stay between the two armies, keep them both at bay, and deal with them, as it suited him, one at a time.

The first thing to do was to beat General Fremont to Strasburg. Stonewall's army covered the eighteen miles in one very hot day, camping that night only three miles away from Fremont. The next day they tried to provoke Fremont into battle, but he wouldn't fight. He needed Shields to help bag Stonewall and Shields wasn't there.

So now Stonewall had to get his army to the lower end of the valley before Shields' troops arrived and before Fremont's could catch up. Marching down the old roads they knew so well, the army kept close to the North Fork of the Shenandoah River so they could destroy bridges along the way and make it harder for the two Union armies to join up. It was a race for time, but Stonewall's men were used to racing. His old brigade called themselves "Jackson's Foot Calvary" and joked about the fact that it had taken forty years for Moses to lead his people through the Wilderness, but if the Old Man had been there, he would have double-quicked them, put them on half rations, and made it in three days.

On June 5th (five days after leaving Winchester) Jackson was at Port Republic at the southern end of the valley, where two small rivers come together to form the Shenandoah River. He sent a cavalry unit up the river to destroy the one bridge on that side which the Union forces might use. Stonewall Jackson was between the two generals now but he was in possession of the only remaining bridge on either river. General Fremont was on the west side; General Shields' forces were on the east with Jackson's artillery trained on them from a mountaintop. The fox was not going to be easy to bag, after all. In fact, neither of the Union generals seemed anxious to fight.

But Stonewall was. The big attack, he decided, would be on June 8th and 9th—first against Shields, then against Fremont. The plan was this: General "Old Baldy" Ewell, who had already engaged Fremont in some initial skirmishing, would put on a big show, pretending that Jackson's whole army was with him on the west side of the river. Actually a large contingent of Ewell's men would be on the other side, helping Stonewall fight Shields. When Shields had been beaten, Stonewall would go to Ewell's aid and together they'd take care of Fremont.

Shields proved, however, to be a tougher adversary than the Confederates had expected, more than Stonewall and his forces could manage alone. In the end Stonewall had to send for Ewell to come to his rescue. Abandoning their own battle, Ewell and his men rushed across the river, but they took care to burn the bridge behind them so Fremont couldn't follow. Then the full force of Jackson's army got to work and forced the Yankees to retreat: Shields up one side of the river, Fremont up the other. The Valley campaign was over.

Stonewall turned to Ewell. "General," he said,

his eyes flashing, "he who does not see the hand of God in this is blind, sir, blind!"

In forty days Stonewall Jackson's army had marched 400 miles, won five battles, defeated three generals, killed or wounded 3,500 men, captured another 3,500 and, most important, they had kept 40,000 Union soldiers from fighting at Richmond.

Jackson's success was so spectacular that the Richmond newspaper declared in large, bold-faced type: "Glorious old Stonewall is fast becoming the HERO OF THE WAR." Stonewall was more than a newspaper hero; he had become a symbol of victory. His story took on a legendary character and even his name seemed to work wonders. "Hush," northern mothers would tell their rambunctious children. "Be good or Stonewall will get you." Stonewall's troops adopted the practice of chanting his name as they charged into battle, "Stonewall Jackson! Stonewall Jackson!" They would fire off the name as if they half expected that it alone would overcome the enemy. They might have been announcing the presence of Jack the Giant Killer or some other invincible character from a fairy tale, and indeed the enemy sometimes responded as if Stonewall were just such a hero. Once a small group of Union soldiers captured by Stonewall were so impressed that they boasted to everyone they passed that they weren't common prisoners. They "had the honor of being captured by Stonewall Jackson himself."

His image was so well fixed in the public mind

that no matter what he did or didn't do, he was still a hero. In actual fact, his conduct in the next campaign was not up to standard; at times it was strange. The campaign was to be at Richmond where General McClellan had his army of 105,000 entrenched in a semi-circle, the right wing extending north, ready to receive reinforcements. Because of the recent wounding of General Johnston, General Robert E. Lee was now in command of the Army of Northern Virginia, and it was this right wing of McClellan's that he planned to attack. Lee had only 80,000 men (including Jackson's), so he had to figure out ways to deceive the enemy. First, he had to fool them into thinking that the main part of his army was still in front of Richmond when actually there would be only a token force there. (He ordered a few troops to march back and forth in different places and make a lot of noise.) Next, he wanted the enemy to think that Jackson was going north rather than south, so he openly sent reinforcements north by train, then secretly sent them back. "Be careful," Lee wrote Stonewall, "to guard from friends and foes your purpose."

Stonewall was never more thorough in his efforts to mystify. He schemed to have false rumors planted in enemy camps. At times he disappeared and his own staff didn't know where he was. Indeed he was so secretive that his generals became irritated. If something happened to Jackson, how could they take over? they asked. "He hasn't any more sense than my horse," one general snapped. Even newly arrived reinforcements were so well coached in secrecy that Jackson himself couldn't pry information from one of them.

A young soldier, breaking ranks to pick cherries, was stopped by Jackson, whom he didn't know.

"Where are you going?" Jackson asked.

"I don't know," the soldier replied.

"What is your name?"

"I don't know."

"What regiment do you belong to?"

"I don't know."

By this time Jackson was annoyed. "What does this mean?" he asked.

"Why, you see," the soldier said, "Old Stonewall gave orders yesterday that we are not to know anything . . . and we mean to obey him."

In the end, however, it was a captured straggler in Jackson's army who let the secret out: Stonewall Jackson was on the way to Richmond. As it turned out, the leaking of this information may have been a lucky accident for the Confederates because it scared McClellan. He believed that the Confederate army was far larger than it really was. His own intelligence agency told him that the Confederates had 200,000 men, twice as many as he had, and he didn't question the figures. He just wanted to be careful. Ever since leaving Washington, he'd been begging Lincoln for reinforcements, but no matter how many new men he received, he never thought he had enough. "Sending men to that army," Lincoln said, "is like shoveling fleas across a barnyard." The plain fact was that McClellan had what Lincoln called "the slows."

And now the news of Stonewall Jackson's imminent arrival seemed to McClellan to be the last straw. Outnumbered as he thought he was, how could he hope to take Richmond if the Confederate army was growing even stronger? On June 25th he cancelled the next day's plans for a small-scale attack and wondered whether he shouldn't move his army away from Richmond altogether, perhaps to a new base on the James River where the Federal fleet was anchored.

Of course McClellan knew that he could not move anywhere without fighting and on June 26th the fighting began at Mechanicsville, a small town north of Richmond. According to Lee's plan, five Confederate generals were to descend on Mechanicsville at an appointed time, wait for a signal from Stonewall Jackson, and then attack in unison. But Stonewall never got there. Eventually the other generals grew impatient and attacked without him. By nightfall Jackson was within sound of the battle, but still he went no farther. Perhaps he didn't realize it *was* a battle; perhaps he thought it was too late for him to help. He had spent a hot, humid day struggling through swampy country, crossing rivers whose bridges had been burned down, stopping to remove road blocks that Union soldiers had set up. In the last four days he'd had a total of four hours of sleep, so perhaps it was impossible for him to do more. But he did not send word to Lee that he was behind schedule and wouldn't be coming; perhaps he simply could not admit that anything was impossible for him. Meanwhile the Confederates lost their battle.

The next day, in spite of his victory, McClellan continued to retreat and Lee continued to pursue. Fighting began in the early afternoon near the town of Gaines Mill, but Jackson was not there and it looked as if the Union forces would win again. But at four o'clock, two hours after the onset of the battle, the news flashed through the Confederate lines: "Jackson is here! Jackson is here!"

Stonewall placed his units at the front and watched the battle as he sucked a lemon. A Confederate soldier described the scene:

"With intense but thoroughly suppressed excitement, Jackson moved to and fro, receiving dispatches, issuing orders . . . in the curt, brief accents that characterized him. . . . Toward dusk a courier galloped up and delivered a message from one of the generals that the 'enemy did not give way.'

"Jackson's eyes glittered under his cap. . . . 'Tell him if they stand at sunset to press them with the bayonet.' "

Eventually, however, the enemy did give way. The entire Confederate line moved forward and the battle was over.

Woh-who-ey! There was no doubt about who had won.

Stonewall Jackson glanced down at the lemon he'd been working on throughout the battle. It was the best lemon he'd ever tasted, he said.

In seven days of successive battles, the Confederates cheered only that once. From Gaines Mill to Harrison's Landing, McClellan's destination on the James River, "there was nothing," according to General Taylor of Louisiana, "but a series of blunders, one after another, and all huge." The countryside was difficult to traverse—swampy, wooded, crisscrossed with swollen streams, alive with flies and mosquitoes. Still, there was no excuse, Taylor contended, for the Confederates to be so ignorant of the terrain. Though the whole district was within a day's march of Richmond, the Confederate commanders, Taylor said, "knew no more about the topography of the country than they did about Central Africa." Various units were forever meeting to ask directions, hiring guides who misled them, losing the enemy and each other.

On June 30th Stonewall Jackson was in an area known as White Oak Swamp. On the other side of the swamp, within earshot, fighting was going on, but Jackson was stopped by a river with no way of crossing it. The one bridge he could have used had been destroyed. He halted, ordered the bridge to be repaired, but he seemed to be in a "peculiar" mood, his officers noted. Instead of hurrying the repair job along as was his habit, Stonewall sat down under a tree and went to sleep. He left no instructions to be awakened. And indeed, when he was informed that the bridge had been fixed, he still made no effort to move. Perhaps if he had known that the Union opposition on the other side of the swamp was commanded by his old enemy from Florida, William French, he might have been aroused. As it was, he seemed vague, indifferent, and he fell asleep at supper with a biscuit between his teeth. He was missed at the fighting, but he never offered an explanation as to what he'd done that day.

General Daniel Hill, Jackson's brother-in-law who was serving with him, said he wasn't surprised at this behavior. Jackson never performed as well under another man as he did when he was in full charge. Undoubtedly, after the intense valley campaign over which he'd had complete control, Jackson experienced both a physical and psychological letdown. Once when it was suggested that he might have helped at White Oak, Jackson became testy. "If General Lee had wanted me, he could have sent for me," he said.

By July 1st Jackson's spirits had apparently recovered, for he led the army to Malvern Hill where McClellan was making his final stand. Again nothing went right. Each of the Confederate units made courageous attacks, but they could never get together for a concerted movement. General Hill said later that the concentration of Federal guns was so great that the result was plain murder. Jackson's command alone lost more than 2,000 men—killed, wounded or missing. And of course, after the Confederates had withdrawn, the generals worried: What if McClellan decided to counterattack the next day? They awakened Stonewall, already asleep on the ground, and informed him of their fears.

Stonewall told them to relax. McClellan would be gone by daylight, he said. And so he was.

By July 4th McClellan was at Harrison's Landing under the protection of the Federal navy. The Confederates had followed him there but decided the Union position was too strong to challenge. The two armies were still drawn up in line for battle, however, when the soldiers themselves decided to call an informal truce. Between the two lines was a field full of blackberries. A Confederate private reported, "So our boys and the Yanks made a bargain not to fire at each other, and went out in the field . . . and gathered berries together and talked over the fight, traded tobacco and coffee and exchanged newspapers as peacefully and kindly as if they had not been engaged for the last seven days in butchering one another."

The seven days of butchering were over now, and although McClellan and his army had escaped, Richmond was safe, for the time being at least. Virginians were too relieved to suggest that their army might have done better. They were free, weren't they?

And they still had Stonewall. People could not seem to get close enough to Stonewall or do enough for him. Just seeing Stonewall was enough to make a person feel he'd earned a place in history. In the recent campaign, for instance, Stonewall had stopped outside a farmhouse for a drink of water. When the woman who had handed him the pitcher heard who he was, she emptied the rest of the water on to the ground. No one would drink from that pitcher again, she said. It would be handed down in the family as the pitcher that Stonewall Jackson had last drunk from.

On another occasion Stonewall, riding Little Sorrel through an oatfield, was stopped by the farmer who owned the field. Who did he think he was? the farmer wanted to know. Tramping down people's oatfields!

One of Stonewall's staff explained that this was General Jackson.

"What! *Stonewall* Jackson?" The farmer turned to Jackson. "General," he said, "do me the honor to ride all over my damned old oats!"

Stonewall couldn't go into Richmond without being mobbed by the public. When he appeared in church, he caused a sensation. Pressed with invitations, deluged with gifts, Stonewall was always courteous, sometimes embarrassed, probably astonished, but if he was secretly proud of being a hero, he tried not to let himself know. And why was God so good to him? Actually, Stonewall's God seemed very much like Stonewall himself. He had strict rules and favored those who obeyed them. And the first rule was to acknowledge that He was in charge.

People should not make heroes of men, Stonewall wrote a friend. Instead, they should give "all the glory to God." Indeed, it was dangerous to do otherwise; success might not continue.

Nine

IF Stonewall Jackson was regarded as unbeatable by the public, the officers who had fought with him around Richmond must have been puzzled. Had his success in the valley been pure luck? Was he unable to perform unless he was in full command? General Lee treated him carefully. Neither publicly nor privately did he ever question Jackson's actions in the seven days of fighting. Instead, he sent him north on an independent mission with instructions to do whatever he thought was best.

A new Union army, 50,000 strong, had been formed, made up of men who had fought in the Shenandoah, who had been stationed near Washington, and some who had been attached to McDowell's forces. In command was General John Pope who boasted that he was so active, he made his headquarters in his saddle. Confederates called him "Pope the Braggart" and pointed out that he made his headquarters where most people put their hindquarters. At the moment Pope's army was divided and Jackson was pursuing the part under the command of his old enemy, General Banks.

The two forces met in August, 1862, at Cedar Mountain between Richmond and Washington, but unfortunately Jackson was in such a hurry to fight that he didn't check the enemy's position carefully enough. He thought they were all on the right (or east) of the road, but it turned out that a large part was on the left where Jackson was least prepared. Yankees swarmed among the Confederates in a huge mix-up that threatened to become a Confederate rout. For a while it looked as if this might be another defeat like the one at Kernstown when General Garnett had ordered a retreat. But Stonewall refused to let that happen. For a man who loved danger for its own sake, this was a battle to glory in. Riding into the thick of the confusion with bullets whizzing by on all sides, he put the full power of his will to work. "Rally, men!" he called. "Where's my Stonewall Brigade? Forward, men, forward!"

The men couldn't resist him. They cheered and gradually did manage somehow to move forward. Reinforcements came up from behind and the course of the battle was reversed.

A Yankee soldier with a broken sword stopped fighting to watch this amazing performance.

"What officer is that?" he asked a Confederate. When he heard who it was, he cried out in spite of himself, "Hurrah for General Jackson! Follow your general, boys!"

After the Cedar Mountain victory, the forces

began to mass on both sides. General McClellan, stripped of much of his power, was ordered to leave the Richmond area and help Pope. Lee was joining Jackson, and although both sides hoped for a final showdown, people were discouraged. This war was more than they had bargained for. Groups of northern Democrats were clamoring for peace; abolitionists were demanding that Lincoln declare that the war was to free the slaves as well as to preserve the Union; moderates were predicting that northern soldiers wouldn't fight if slavery were the issue. Some wouldn't fight anyway. Thousands were escaping to Canada and Europe to avoid being drafted. In order to discourage deserting in the Confederate ranks, on several occasions Lee had runaways shot in front of their own units.

Still, most of the men on both sides just kept marching. One tired soldier from Louisiana wrote home; "Jackson travels too much for me. I can't stand this kind of life."

Although they didn't know it yet, the two armies would meet again within a few weeks at Manassas where they had first faced each other thirteen months ago. But before this, Jackson was to take his men behind Pope's army in an effort to cut off the enemy's supply and communication bases. Many of the men had already walked through their shoe leather and were barefooted, yet they had fifty miles to cover in two days and all they had to eat was raw corn and green apples picked along the way. Still, near the end of their journey when Stonewall stopped to watch the troops go by, they began to cheer as usual. Afraid that the enemy would be aroused, Stonewall motioned them to be quiet. So as they filed past their general, they raised their hats, waved them in the air, and grinned.

Stonewall waved back. "Who could not conquer with such troops as these?" he asked.

In the end the men may have decided that the long march was worthwhile. After they had wrecked the enemy's railroad, they took possession of their warehouses which turned out to be full of food. At first they were told not to touch the food, but when news came that Pope was advancing, Jackson told his men to help themselves. Take all they could carry, he said, and burn the rest. Woh-who-ey! It was like turning children loose in a candy store where the candy was free. It was curious, a lieutenant reported, to see a starving man, barefooted and in tatters, feasting on lobster salad and fancy wine. "Some filled their haversacks with cakes, some candy, other oranges, lemons, canned goods." One man took nothing but French mustard which he subsequently traded off for meat and bread.

Four days later (August 29th) they were all at Manassas and in battle again. It was as if nothing had happened during the last year and they were beginning the war over again, fighting on the same ground, killing and killing to make sure there was death enough. As usual, the Union army had more men. They flung themselves at the Confederates, wave after wave. When their cartridges ran out, they still came on. The two sides resorted to bayonets, clubbed each other with the butt end of their muskets, and when all else failed, picked up stones and threw them. The Confederate line held, but one set of Yankees replaced another as if their supply of men were endless. At last General A. P. Hill, at the center of the assaults, sent word to Jackson that his men might not be able to beat back the next wave.

"Tell him . . . they *must*," Jackson replied.

The sun climbed the afternoon sky as Stonewall rode among his troops.

"Can you stand it just two more hours, men? Just two hours." Then it was an hour that Stonewall was asking for. Then half an hour. When Hill finally pushed the enemy back, Stonewall said he knew he would do it.

It had, however, been a long day. "No one knows how long sixty seconds are," one officer wrote, "nor how much time can be crowded into an hour. . . unless he has been under the fire of a desperate battle, holding on . . . hour after hour, minute after minute . . . praying that the great red sun, blazing and motionless overhead, would go down."

There was a total of 25,000 casualties (15,000 Union; 10,000 Confederate), but in spite of the year between the two battles at Manassas, the Union army retired almost as disorganized as it had the first time. McClellan never supplied Pope with all the men he should have, but nevertheless President Lincoln put McClellan back in command and sent

Pope west. It was clear that Pope did not have the confidence of the army, and McClellan, though he might suffer from "the slows," did.

Pope, Banks, Fremont, Shields, Milroy—they had all passed, a Confederate soldier observed, but "the star of Jackson mounted toward the zenith," and, he said, "it was the star of victory."

Certainly the morale of the Confederates was high after Manassas. If ever Jackson and Lee had secret doubts about each other, they were gone now. Lee treated Jackson as a partner and together they agreed that this was the time to take the war into the north. If they invaded Maryland, they might pick up volunteers from this border state where sympathies were mixed. Moreover, if they won a victory on northern soil, they might persuade England and France to recognize the Confederacy officially as a separate nation and give it support.

On September 16th the Confederate army marched into Frederick, Maryland, where they set up their headquarters. They did not make an impressive appearance. According to one Maryland boy, they were the dirtiest men he had ever seen, "a most ragged, lean and hungry set of wolves." Yet there was "a dash about them," the boy admitted, "that the northern men lacked. They rode like circus riders." Few men in Maryland, however, volunteered to join this ragged outfit. What was worse, more than 10,000 Confederates never crossed into northern territory. Some had simply dropped behind; some refused to fight on northern soil. They'd agreed to defend the South, they said, and they'd wait until the war came back there.

Lee's plans were not proceeding well at all. He had expected Union troops occupying Harpers Ferry to be withdrawn in order to participate in the battle that was obviously shaping up in Maryland. Certainly he didn't want the 10,000 Yankees at Harpers Ferry to be at his back in a battle, so when he heard they were still there, he sent Jackson to take care of them. He wrote out Order No. 191 which contained the plans for various units and he sent a copy to each of his generals.

Somehow the copy that went to General D. H. Hill wound up in the hands of a staff officer. For some reason the staff officer used the piece of paper to wrap around some cigars, and when the Confederate army moved out of Frederick, the staff officer happened to drop those cigars and that piece of paper out of his pocket and on to the ground. And when McClellan's army moved into Frederick a few days later—there they lay, right in the path of a Union soldier. More interested in the cigars than the paper, the soldier might have tossed the paper away, but he didn't. He read it, recognized its importance, and delivered it to General McClellan.

Meanwhile Stonewall Jackson was taking Harpers Ferry with a minimum of opposition. He placed his artillery in the hills that circled the city and arranged to have them all fired at the same time. When Union guns replied, they were knocked out of commission by Jackson's batteries carefully positioned in the territory that he knew so well. The Union garrison, bombarded from all sides, soon decided that resistance was useless and surrendered. Jackson rode into town through lines of gawking Yankees, straining to catch a glimpse of the famous Stonewall. "Many of them saluted as he passed," a staff officer wrote, "and he invariably returned the salute. I heard one of the men say . . . 'Boys, he's not much for looks, but if we'd had him, we wouldn't have been caught in this trap.' "

But Jackson wasted little time in Harpers Ferry. He had heard from Lee that the Confederates were in trouble. McClellan, miraculously cured of his "slows" after reading the cigar paper, was on the way to Sharpsburg, Maryland, the place that Lee had designated for the Confederates to meet. If McClellan caught Lee's troops before the others arrived, there would obviously be a disaster. So Jackson left the details of the Harpers Ferry surrender to General A. P. Hill and he hurried to join Lee.

On September 16th, while Jackson was pushing toward Sharpsburg, Lee had his small army of 20,000 stretched in a thin line along Antietam Creek. His army had never been smaller, and even with the remaining 20,000 (divided between Jackson and A. P. Hill) which had not yet arrived from Harpers Ferry, he would have only half as many men as McClellan. If McClellan had attacked on September 16th, he would without question have wiped out the Confederates then and there, but for some incredible reason McClellan was still convinced that the Confederates outnumbered him. So on September 16th he took his time, reviewed his tactics, looked through his field glasses, talked to his generals. He did not move until the morning of September 17th and by then Jackson and his men had arrived and were posted on high ground in a cornfield on the Confederate left.

It was this cornfield that McClellan chose to attack first. Three times his men took the cornfield; three times they were driven back while the dead bodies piled up and the corn began to look, as one soldier said, "as if it had been struck by a storm of bloody hail." At noon the two lines were in the same position they had been in at the start of the battle: no ground gained, no ground lost, only blood shed—so much blood that a Union soldier said that at one point the whole landscape turned red and swam before his eyes.

The day came to be known as the bloodiest in the war—"a great tumbling together of heaven and earth," a Wisconsin man called it. McClellan abandoned his efforts in the cornfield and turned his attention to the center of Lee's line. Here he had more success. After repeated attacks, he broke the line and had he pushed on, he might have finished off the battle. But McClellan had the habit of stopping just short of victory. Now he imagined a counterattack might develop from those non-existent Confederate reserves that he believed were waiting somewhere in the wings, so he concentrated on a new position. He ordered General Ambrose Burnside to move his forces to a hill across the creek where he could train his guns on the Confederates.

Stonewall Jackson stayed on the left, sending units back and forth to reinforce danger spots, using the few men available to the best advantage. Yet it was a strange day for Stonewall—not one that required a hero, for these were hardened, determined veterans who needed no rallying cries. They would fight around the bodies of their fallen comrades, fight until they themselves fell before they would give an inch. Stonewall sat in an unusually relaxed manner on the back of Little Sorrel, eating peaches and issuing orders. He said afterward that in the midst of all that killing, he had somehow known that nothing would happen to him. He had been possessed by an extraordinary feeling of absolute safety that he'd never experienced before. It was his personal safety that he felt sure of, not the army's; so along with everyone else, he kept an anxious watch on the road to Sharpsburg. If General A. P. Hill and his men would arrive from Harpers Ferry, there might still be a chance to stop General Burnside before it was too late.

By midafternoon Burnside had barely established himself in the hills when General A. P. Hill in his bright red battle shirt came dashing down the road, his 3,000 men behind him. It wasn't a large force, considering the strength of the opposition, but it was enough. Burnside pulled back his men; the day ended, and so did the battle. Both sides claimed to have won a victory, but in most

respects it was a draw. With 10,000 Confederate soldiers lost and 12,000 Union, the real winners were simply the survivors, though many were too sickened by the sights of the day to rejoice in anything. "No tongue can tell, no mind conceive, no pen portray the horrible sights I witnessed this morning," a Pennsylvania soldier wrote. "Of this war I am heartily sick and tired."

The next day McClellan had another chance to wipe out the Confederates, for they remained in Sharpsburg twenty-four hours longer, but McClellan did not move. Nor did he move when Lee returned to Virginia, although again had he been aggressive, he might have ended the war. "Destroy the rebel army, if possible," Lincoln ordered McClellan, and when he didn't, Lincoln began looking around for another general.

With no further interference from the Yankees, the Confederates settled down in Virginia to reorganize and reinforce themselves. Jackson was given command of the Second Corps with 34,000 men under him and on October 11th he was made a lieutenant general, about as far up the ladder as an officer could go. For a man who once thought rank was all-important and who wanted, above all, to be "noticed," Jackson had certainly gone further than he (or anyone else) could ever have imagined.

His former students at Lexington must have been astonished to see Old Jack not only a military hero but the idol of young women, the rage of the day. Indeed there seemed to be no lengths to which the ladies would not go for a memento or just a glimpse of their beloved Stonewall. On one occasion they broke the shutters of his hotel room, forced open the windows, and threw red and white roses at his feet. When he finally invited them in, they fought, squealing and laughing, to hold his hands, begged for autographs, and tore the buttons off his coat for souvenirs. One lady boasted that she had a bracelet made of the hair from Little Sorrel's tail. Another treasured a scarf that Little Sorrel had stepped on. In the midst of such attention, Stonewall could find nothing to say but "thank you, thank you," but when the ladies asked for locks of his hair, he managed a firm "no."

So Stonewall was certainly noticed. And now he was a lieutenant-general. When he wrote Anna the news, he followed it with what may have seemed a surprising question. He wondered if he had made a mistake in the choice of a career. Perhaps he should have been a Christian minister; wasn't this the highest of all professions? Stonewall had reached the summit of his career and he was asking himself, where could he go now? In addition, he must have wondered what the rank of lieutenant general meant in the eyes of God. Would not God have placed him in a higher bracket if he had been a minister of the gospel? Success had not satisfied that knot of ambition in Stonewall Jackson; it had, if anything, hardened it.

General Taylor of Louisiana would have recognized these questions for what they were. He once gave his opinion of Jackson's character. "Observing him closely," he said, "I caught a glimpse of the man's inner nature. It was but a glimpse, yet in that moment I saw an ambition boundless as Cromwell's, and as merciless. . . . His ambition was vast, all-absorbing. . . . He loathed it, perhaps feared it, but he could not escape it—it was himself. . . . He fought it with prayer, constant and earnest." Surely his thoughts about the ministry were part both of his ambition and of his desperate fight against it.

Ten

*F*IVE *days after the Battle of Antietam, President* Lincoln issued a proclamation, stating that on January 1st he would declare that all slaves in rebellious states were free. Since slaves in states loyal to the Union were not affected and since the seceding or rebellious states would certainly not abide by anything Lincoln said, his proclamation might not seem to amount to much, yet people in both the north and the south understood that the character of the war had changed.

Up to this time northerners had said they were fighting to preserve the Union; now whether they liked it or not, they were also fighting to free slaves. So if any southerners still hoped for a peaceful settlement of differences, they gave that up quickly. This would be a war to the bitter end unless, of course, the Confederates surrendered before January 1, 1863, when the Emancipation Proclamation was to take effect. Southerners did not give that any thought at all, although they realized that Europeans were against slavery and it would be difficult for them to give the Confederacy official recognition now that slavery, rather than simple independence, had become an issue. This was a serious disadvantage since the south did not have the resources of the north and would have liked support from Europe. But at least the south did have the generals. As one Confederate soldier said, "Old Jack can do it without resources."

At the moment the Confederates were building up manpower. In the three months between Antietam and the next battle, Lee's army expanded from 30,000 to 75,000. While Jackson kept busy trying to supply his corps with new equipment, that dashing cavalryman, General Jeb Stuart, decided to supply Jackson with a much-needed new coat. Worried about the buttons the ladies kept taking from Stonewall's shabby old uniform, General Stuart had a fancy new coat delivered to Jackson's quarters. It had shiny brass buttons, a satin lining, and gold lace. Jackson looked at it in awe, touching it gingerly as if it were the skin of an exotic animal. It was, of course, just the kind of flashy outfit that Jeb Stuart would wear, but Stonewall shook his head. It didn't suit him, he told the staff officer who delivered it. It "is too handsome for me," he said, "but I shall prize it highly as a souvenir." He started to put it away but the staff officer asked him to try it on so he could report to General Stuart on the fit.

So Stonewall put on the coat and was persuaded to keep it on for dinner which was about to be served outdoors. Stepping out of his tent in his new finery, Stonewall created a sensation, not only among his staff but in the entire camp. Word spread quickly: Old Jack was dressed up in gold lace! Come and see! Soldiers came running by the hundreds; who would want to miss such a spectacle? After dinner Stonewall put the coat away but he did consent to have another uniform made up out of a roll of gray cloth that had been sent him as a gift.

Army morale was high but no higher than Jackson's own spirits. He often thought that God must hold him in high favor indeed to have brought him safely through so much danger, to have given him so many friends and admirers, and to have made him so successful in war. Moreover, Jackson had received good news from North Carolina. After spending the winter in Winchester with Stonewall, Anna had returned to her family and wrote that she was expecting a baby. Jackson could scarcely have been happier.

There was, however, even more cause to be grateful. Throughout the south there was a sudden revival in religion. People who had neglected going to church began attending again. Huge crowds were pouring into tent meetings conducted by traveling ministers. Soldiers were gathering to sing hymns and pray not just on Sundays but on week nights as well. It was as if God, Himself, had come to the South to prepare it for victory. Indeed, religious and patriotic feelings often seemed to run in the same current. Filled with such feelings, Stonewall was walking back one night from a tent meeting when all at once a group of soldiers in one area of camp let loose with the wonderful rebel yell. Woh-who-ey! It was the cry of victory piercing the night air, letting the whole world know that the south was right and the south would win. Scarcely had the sound died down when it was taken up in another quarter, and so it traveled throughout the camp like an echo receding, repeating, asserting itself, on and on in the dark.

Stonewall leaned against a fence and listened until the last note had faded away. "That was the sweetest music I ever heard," he said.

How could an army capable of such a spontaneous expression of unity not be victorious in the end? The end, however, seemed far away and Stonewall was restless. So was President Lincoln. On November 9th he appointed General Ambrose Burnside to replace McClellan. Burnside, a modest man with bushy whiskers (cheek whiskers have been called sideburns in his honor ever since), did not want the job, even though he'd always been interested in military tactics. As a boy, the son of an Indiana tailor, he used to arrange buttons in military formation and then put them through complicated operations. Once he had used five hundred buttons, but it was men, not buttons, he would be dealing with now and at times, he said, he "trembled at the thought."

Still, he had to come up with a campaign plan

quickly. Since McClellan had failed to take Richmond by using the water route, Burnside decided to march overland, crossing the Rappahannock River at Fredericksburg, Virginia, midway between Washington and Richmond. Lincoln approved the idea but reminded Burnside that he must move quickly across the Rappahannock before Lee and Jackson, camped in northern Virginia, could reach him. Burnside promised to move so quickly that he'd be in Richmond for Christmas dinner.

Accordingly, he ordered pontoon bridges to be sent to Fredericksburg so they'd be there when he arrived, ready to take his army across the river. On November 15th he left Warrenton, Virginia (fifty miles west of Washington) and arrived in the hills across from Fredericksburg on November 19th. But the pontoon bridges were not there. Furthermore, when Burnside rode his horse, Major, down to the river, he saw that there were already gray-coated figures on the other side. General Longstreet's Confederate corps had arrived the same day and General Lee was due the next day. Still, Burnside might have taken Fredericksburg if he could have crossed that river then and there. The Confederates had not had time to build up their defenses and Jackson would not arrive for five more days.

Meanwhile the people of Fredericksburg watched the hills across the river fill up with Yankees. They were used to Yankees; the town had been occupied off and on during the last year, but this was obviously not going to be just another occupation; this would be war. Rumors flew around the town; people trained their field glasses on the activity across the river; schoolchildren left their desks and stared out the windows.

The pontoons arrived on November 25th, but somehow the quickness had slipped out of Burnside. He could, of course, have changed his plans when he saw the Confederate gun emplacements going up, the trenches being dug, the troops gathering. But Burnside had said he would go to Richmond through Fredericksburg; he had his buttons arranged that way and that's what he intended to do. Even if winter did come early, even if the ground was covered with snow. No matter what, he'd go through with his plans.

On the night of December 10th a woman's voice from across the river called to Confederate pickets in Fredericksburg. "Yankees cooking big rations! MARCH TOMORROW!" At dawn the next day the Union army turned its cannon on the town, at times firing one hundred guns a minute. Walls toppled, buildings burst into flames, and families rushed to their cellars for safety. At one o'clock in the afternoon the firing stopped long enough for one young girl, whose house had been hit three times, to venture outside. She found her family's garden strewn with cannon balls, their trees stripped of branches, their grape arbor wrecked. During the lull she was hustled out of town, along with all the women and children of Fredericksburg.

"I never saw such a pitiful procession," one observer wrote. "I saw little children trudging along with their doll babies, holding their feet up carefully above the snow, and women so old and feeble that they . . . could barely hobble."

After the bombardment, the Union soldiers crossed the river on their pontoons. A Mississippi unit defended the shore until seven in the evening and then the Confederates left the town to the Yankees. They went into the long line of low hills behind the town where they had prepared their defense and waited for the battle the next day. Meanwhile the Yankees (stragglers mostly) raced like madmen through empty Fredericksburg homes, destroying everything they could lay their hands on. They chopped up furniture, crashed chinaware, bayoneted mirrors, slashed pictures, tore up books, ripped open feather mattresses, and watered their horses in pianos.

At "earliest dawn" the next morning Stonewall Jackson mounted Little Sorrel, but this was not the Old Jack that the army knew. Stonewall was decked out in Jeb Stuart's fancy coat; a new gold-braided hat sat on his head; his huge boots were polished to a gloss. His soldiers gaped, cheered, but they also worried. "Old Jack will be afraid of his clothes," one man grumbled, "and will not get down to work." But as soon as the men saw the Union army marching toward them, they were glad that Stonewall had dressed up. Those Yankees didn't look as if they'd ever been dirty. Their uniforms spic and span, their pennants flying, they came on slowly in straight lines, left–right, left–

right, regular as a clockbeat. It was as if they were so sure of themselves, they felt no need to hurry or even fall out of step. They concentrated first on the Confederate right where Jackson's men were stationed.

Hugging the ground, the Confederates held their fire and waited for the moment when they could inflict the most damage. At eight hundred yards when they could distinguish the faces of the Yankees, they fired—fourteen heavy guns at one time. The Union line staggered, re-formed, came on again, received more artillery fire, backed up, came ahead until they were in range of the muskets, but only in one boggy spot did Jackson's men give ground and then only briefly.

With 113,000 men at his disposal (against Lee's 75,000), Burnside could, of course, attack various points simultaneously. The strongest position on the entire Confederate front was held by General Longstreet at Marye's Heights, just west of town. Thousands of riflemen stood six deep, safely entrenched in a sunken road behind a thick stone wall, ready to fire on any troops foolish enough to venture across the half mile of bare fields before it. "A chicken cannot live on that field when we open on it," a Confederate engineer predicted and indeed no one expected the Yankees to pick the most forbidding spot in Fredericksburg for their most sustained attack.

Yet at twelve noon, just as the Confederate riflemen at Marye's Heights had finished a lunch of hard crackers and were lighting up their pipes, they saw the Yankees coming from town, running doublequick on to that empty field, shouting as they came, "Hi! Hi! Hi!"

A rifleman from Louisiana described the scene: "At once our guns began their deadly work ... How beautifully they came on! Their bright bayonets glistening in the sunlight made the line look like a huge serpent of blue and steel ... We could see our shells bursting their ranks, making great gaps; but on they came. ... Now we gave them cannister, and that staggered them. ... Another line appeared, again recoiled under cannister and fell back in confusion. Little patches of blue lay all over the fields. ... It appeared to us that there was no end. On they came in beautiful array ... but our fire was murderous."

Burnside, watching his doomed troops cut down hour after hour, didn't seem to know what to do except to send more troops after them. "Go back, go back," the Union men called to their reinforcements, but they'd been told to come and on they came. It was sundown before the killing stopped. A whitewashed brick house standing near the stone wall had been hit so often, the whitewash had been entirely knocked off. An iron stove lying on the ground before the house was pockmarked with bullets. All through the battle that stove had sputtered as the bullets hit. Ping! Ping! Ping! It sounded as if it were marking a score in a child's game. And in the field before the sunken road lay the dead and wounded bodies of thousands of Union men. "It was a great slaughter pen," a Union survivor wrote. "They might as well have tried to take Hell."

Incredibly, Burnside wanted to renew the attack on Marye's Heights the next day but his generals talked him out of it, so although the Union army, dead and living, was still in town, nothing much happened. That night Burnside applied for a truce in order to bury the dead. The men assigned to the task said they would give their fallen comrades starlight for their burial, but as it turned out, they received something far more spectacular. Northern lights appeared in the sky, an unusual spectacle for this part of the country, and the dead were buried beneath "banners of flame, columns of pearly light, garlands and wreaths of gold" as if heaven itself had recognized that these brave men deserved a special farewell.

As for Stonewall Jackson, he had not wanted the battle to end when it did. After the assault on Marye's Heights, he was determined to launch an attack, to drive the enemy into the river. His plan hadn't worked out, but then Stonewall always wanted to carry a battle a step farther, to pursue a defeated enemy, to use every opportunity to reduce the number of fighting Yankees. Once when a captain from Alabama had rebuked his men for killing an unusually gallant Union officer, Jackson had objected. "No, Captain," he said. "The men are right. Kill the brave ones. They lead on the others." Stonewall would have agreed with Lincoln when he said that winning a war depended upon being able "to face the arithmetic."

When the Battle of Fredericksburg was over on December 15th, the total arithmetic was in favor of the Confederates. (Union casualties—12,653; Confederate—5,309) After Union troops had withdrawn, the two armies began to settle down for the winter, one on each side of the river. The citizens of Fredericksburg trickled back to town, cleaning up the destruction as they could. General Jackson had suffered from an earache throughout the battle, so although he normally slept in a tent, he accepted the hospitality of the Corbin family whose home lay just south of Fredericksburg. Eventually he moved into a three room office which stood in front of the Corbin residence and which became his headquarters for an unusually cold season.

At the Union campgrounds, the *New York Times* reported, "Certainly never were a graver, gloomier, more sober, sombre, serious and unmusical body of men than the Army of the Potomac at the present time." Walt Whitman, the poet, went to the Union camp to see his brother and reported that "Every one of the soldiers to a man wants to go home." The men were angry. The officers were critical of Burnside, and the soldiers, disgusted at the futility of what they had been through, felt they had more in common with the soldiers across the river than they had with their own command. They would fight like fury, of course, when they had to, but between battles rival soldiers felt little animosity toward each other. They were all in the same fix, weren't they? Homesick, cold, bored, scratching around for a plug of tobacco, scrounging for an extra bit of food. So at Fredericksburg Yankee and Confederate soldiers began calling to each other across the river. They strung rope between the shores and set up a ferry system so they could trade provisions back and forth.

"Hey, Johnny Reb," a Yankee soldier would call.

"Yea, Yank."

"Got any tobacco?"

"Yes, want to trade?"

"Half a pound of coffee for two plugs of tobacco, Reb."

"Right, send it over."

By the end of December the Yankees had recovered sufficiently from their glooms to become musical. On Christmas Eve a Union band performed for their soldiers on one side of the river and on the other side a Confederate band performed for theirs. The Union band started off with what they considered their national anthem, "The Battle Hymn of the Republic." When they finished, the Confederate band played "Dixie" while the Yankees listened. Then spontaneously the two bands struck up the same tune. They didn't need to confer; they simply played while men on both sides joined in singing "Home, Sweet Home."

❧❧ Eleven

STONEWALL *Jackson was almost as secretive about his personal life as he was about his military plans.* On November 24th on the way to Fredericksburg, he had received word that Anna had given birth to a baby girl. Oh, how thankful he was! he wrote Anna. Oh, how happy! But he confided the news to few, if any, of his friends. At Anna's request, he decided on a name— Julia, after his mother. At first, however, he could hardly think of the baby as anything but an "it." "Do not spoil it," he cautioned Anna, "and don't let anybody tease it. Don't permit it to have a bad temper." For Stonewall, of course, it was never too early to introduce rules, but he didn't dwell on them. "How I would love to see the darling little thing," he added. A few days later he asked Anna to tell the baby that he loved her "better than all the baby boys in the world."

But, as always, Jackson felt the danger in too much happiness. Just before the Battle of Fredericksburg, he warned Anna, "Do not set your affections upon her, except as a gift from God. If she absorbs too much of our hearts, God may remove her from us."

Once he was settled in his winter quarters, he looked forward to a visit from Anna and Julia, but the baby was too young and the weather too cool to risk it yet. Meanwhile he consoled himself with visits from five-year-old Janie Corbin, daughter of his hostess, who adopted Stonewall as her special friend. Every afternoon she would wait for his staff to leave and then run over to play with him. Generally, Stonewall had an apple for her and he might take her on his knee and tell her a story, or he might give her his gold-braided hat, which she admired, to try on, or he might let her sit at his desk and work with scissors and paper. Janie liked to cut out rows of paper soldiers. If she folded the paper many times in just the right way and then cut out a figure of a soldier, she would have, when she unfolded it, a long row of paper soldiers, all holding hands. They were the Stonewall Brigade, she said, and though she tried to teach the General how to do it, he never got the hang of it. But one day, to her delight, he cut the gold braid off his hat and tied it around her curls. The braid looked better on her, he said, than it did on him.

Stonewall was different that winter; Anna noticed it too when she came. He was even more religious than usual and stricter than he'd ever been with his men. It was as if he not only had to toughen up his corps for the spring offensive but he had to convince God to join in an all-out effort for victory. This time, he said, "we must do more than defeat their armies; we must destroy them." When an officer was caught stealing a chicken, Stonewall had him stripped of his commission and put in the ranks. He protested that soldiers should be punished, not just reprimanded, for gambling. When leniency was recommended in the case of three enlisted men sentenced to be shot for desertion, Jackson objected. General A. P. Hill said Jackson was a "slumbering volcano"; no one knew when he would erupt.

He was, of course, strict with himself, following not only the spirit but the letter of the law, as he had always done. Once when General Lee sent a messenger, asking to see Jackson at his convenience, Jackson replied that he would be there the next morning. A violent snowstorm came up in the night and continued into the next day, but although Lee's headquarters was fourteen miles away, Jackson did not postpone his visit. He had said he would come, and though time was not that important, he did come. Had people in Clarksburg heard that story, they would not have been surprised. That was just like Tom, they would have said.

During that long winter, the snow caused hardship but it also provided one of the few diversions for the Confederate army. Many of the men from the deep south had never seen snow before and behaved as if they had to make up for lost time. Once 2,500 men took part in a giant snowball fight started by the Georgians. The men filled their haversacks with snowballs and staged a real battle; when they ran out of ammunition, they stepped to the rear and made some more. One soldier (a better fighter than speller) wrote in his diary: "Louisianians came over and gave us a chalenge for a snow ball fight. Battle lasted a couple of hours . . . Whiped them." That was one way to practice for the spring campaign.

General Burnside, however, was not sure that he would wait until spring. He had felt so guilty about the fiasco at Fredericksburg that he had published a letter in which he took full blame, but in January he decided to redeem himself. He'd cross the Rappahannock farther north and make a surprise attack on the enemy. On the night of January 20th, he had his army on the road when it started to rain. This was no ordinary rain. For thirty solid hours it poured while the roads turned to mud so deep that a man trying to take a step sank up to his knees. Teams of mules were buried in the mud; wagons, cannon, pontoons were stuck fast in the road. "So the army comes dragging back," a soldier reported, "in the deep mud and drizzling rain to its old quarters." Union men called it the "Mud March" and it was the end of any offensive until spring.

It was also the end of General Burnside as commander of the Army of the Potomac. Lincoln put Burnside's severest critic, General "Fighting" Joe Hooker, in his place. Many people in the north found it encouraging to have a man in charge known as "Fighting" Joe; most didn't know that his nickname was an accident—the result of a misprint in a newspaper. Lincoln gave him the job because he had done well in the battles around Richmond, and at Antietam he'd kept on fighting after he'd been shot in the foot. Still, Lincoln had misgivings. Almost as soon as Hooker took command, he began boasting that he had "the finest army on the planet" and that his plans were "perfect." When he referred to his spring campaign, he had the habit of saying, "When I take Richmond." It was not only the overconfidence of saying "when" that worried Lincoln but the fact that he was talking about taking Richmond when he should have been planning to destroy the Confederate army. Was this another general who didn't understand arithmetic?

The Confederates and Yankees watched each other closely all winter. Once when some Yankees heard Confederate soldiers raising a cheer, they called: "What's going on over there, Johnny?"

"General Stonewall Jackson!" the Confederates called back, and the Yankees joined in. "Hurrah for General Jackson!" they cried.

Certainly the Confederates must have had their field glasses out during the few days that President Lincoln came to the Union camp to review the troops. What they couldn't see, they would have heard—bugles, drums, tramping feet. And one cold morning a few Confederates had a close-up view of the president, himself. Ten-year-old Tad, the president's son, wanted to see what the enemy looked like, so Lincoln in his tall stovepipe hat,

Tad, and several aides walked to the banks of the Rappahannock and for several minutes watched the gray-coated pickets marching back and forth.

From time to time General Hooker put on a show of great activity. He "is trying what frightening will do," General Lee wrote to his daughter. "He runs out his guns, starts his wagons and troops up and down the river, and creates an excitement generally. Our men look on in wonder, give a cheer, and all subsides."

But no one expected an offensive until the weather improved and spring was slow in coming. Bluebirds came back to Virginia in February, a month ahead of their normal schedule, but they were a false alarm. Rain and cold continued through March and were accompanied by sickness. General Lee was in a serious condition for a while and little Janie Corbin died of scarlet fever. Stonewall, who never flinched at the sight of death on the battlefield, wept at the loss of Janie. Indeed it seemed as if winter and the war were in league and both would go on forever. The Union army sent its much celebrated observation balloon to hang over the Confederate camp and report on activities, but there was no more to see on one side of the river than on the other. Cold men went about their duties in cold weather. Snow fell even in April but at last the peach and cherry trees showed promise of blooming and Stonewall sent for Anna and Julia. They arrived on April 20th in the midst of a rainstorm.

The three Jacksons would have just nine days

together. Stonewall kept his normal working routine but spent every free moment enjoying his family, showing Anna his vast collection of gifts, and admiring Julia. He would hold her up in front of a mirror. "Now, Miss Jackson," he would say, "look at yourself." He also took on the task of disciplining her. He had written Anna that she must not allow Julia to be willful, so when Julia cried in his arms, Stonewall put her down and would not pick her up until she had quieted. He "stood over her with as much coolness and determination," Anna said, "as if he were directing a battle." Anna glowed with approval for everything her husband did. He was thirty-nine years old now and Anna said she had never seen him so healthy and handsome. Indeed he was, in her words, the very "impersonation of fearlessness and manly vigor."

His manly vigor was to be called upon all too soon. On the morning of April 29th Jackson was awakened by a messenger: Hooker was crossing the river. The spring campaign had started and Anna and Julia must leave at once. Stonewall made arrangements for their departure, said a hasty good-bye, and met with General Lee. Waiting for reports on enemy activity from Jeb Stuart and his scouts, the two generals stood on an observation hill and discussed what should be done.

Meanwhile General Hooker was carrying out what he called his "perfect" plan. He had put his finger on a map and told his associates, "Gentlemen, if I can put my army there, God Almighty can't drive me out." His finger lay on a road crossing

known as Chancellorsville (only a house, not a town), twenty-five miles northwest of Fredericksburg. He planned to leave part of his forces in Fredericksburg and take the major part of his army north, crossing both the Rappahannock and Rapidan rivers, and then circling back to Chancellorsville. In this way the Confederates would be caught between his troops. The only thing they could do, he said, would be to retreat to Richmond, and even to do this, they would be in an exposed position. "I have Lee in one hand," Hooker gloated, "and Richmond in the other." Indeed, Hooker believed it was such a good plan, a battle would hardly have to be fought. Lee would see the helplessness of his situation and run off to Richmond while "Fighting" Joe Hooker would have won the spring offensive without losing any, or at least not many, men. What could be more perfect?

As soon as Lee was informed of the enemy position, he understood that he was at a disadvantage. Not even all his troops were at hand. General Longstreet had taken a contingent south of Richmond to scout for food and supplies. So Lee had only 60,000 men against Hooker's 130,000 and he saw at once that Hooker expected him to retreat. But he wouldn't do it. Instead, he divided his small army, just as Hooker had done. Leaving part behind in Fredericksburg, Lee and Jackson took the rest up the road toward Chancellorsville.

On May 1st the two armies met, and when Hooker, in his headquarters at Chancellorsville, heard the firing, he realized, of course, that Lee was not following his "perfect" plan. It seemed impossible that Lee would be foolish enough to fight against such odds. Did Lee have more men than Hooker knew about? Did he have a secret plan that Hooker had not thought of? The longer he listened to the firing, the more reports he heard about the battle, the more nervous Hooker became. At one o'clock in the afternoon, he could stand it no longer. He ordered all his forces to retreat and take a defensive position around Chancellorsville.

The Union men were doing so well ("in a splendid position and driving the enemy," according to a colonel from Massachusetts) that at first they couldn't believe the order. When it became clear that Hooker really meant what he'd said, the whole army was disgusted. General Meade, who had to abandon the high ground he held, could scarcely contain himself. "If he can't hold the top of a hill," he fumed, "how does he expect to hold the bottom of it?"

By evening the army was entrenched in its new position around Chancellorsville, waiting for the Confederates to take the initiative the next day. General Lee surveyed the situation, saw that a frontal attack would be futile, and returned to headquarters to consult with Jackson. While they were talking, General Jeb Stuart arrived with the report that the right wing of the Union army was camped about five miles west of Chancellorsville in an exposed position, perfect for a surprise attack if it could be managed.

Lee and Jackson stepped into the woods where

they could talk alone. Sitting on two large cracker boxes, they discussed the possibilities, going over a map that had been provided by a local guide. There was an old woodcutter's road that wound through the forest, out of sight much of the time. It would lead eventually to better roads, ending up just where they wanted to be: under cover of trees behind the enemy and ready to take it by surprise. Of course it was a risky business. Hidden though the road might be, it was still across the front of the Union army, yet there seemed to be no alternative except retreat. Lee suggested that he would stay behind with 14,000 men to divert the enemy. Would Jackson like to be in charge of the secret attack?

This was, of course, exactly the kind of challenge that Stonewall enjoyed most. Outnumbered two to one, the Confederate army, already divided (part in Fredericksburg), would divide again, not to defend itself but to attack! For a man who liked to prove that nothing was impossible, this was the chance of a lifetime. Indeed this seemed to be the answer to Jackson's winter-long prayers. If this maneuver did not end the war, it might at least decide it. Lee and Jackson completed their plans, spread saddle blankets on the ground and, using their saddles as pillows, they went to sleep.

Jackson woke up early the next morning with a cold but he scarcely noticed it. By eight o'clock he had his men, 28,000 of them, on the march, a column six miles long twisting through the woods, faster and faster but never quite fast enough for

Jackson. "Never can I forget the eagerness and intensity of Jackson on that march," an officer wrote later. "His face was pale, his eyes flashing . . . He leaned over the neck of his horse as if in that way the march might be hurried." Hour after hour as the sun burned away the daylight, Stonewall with tight-lipped concentration urged his men to press forward, press forward. He spoke in the quick, clipped way he always used in times of stress, as if he were firing every word out of the barrel of a musket.

Such a long column of men could not pass completely unnoticed. Yankee pickets saw them and reported it to headquarters. Hooker was delighted. His plan was proceeding perfectly, he said; the Confederates were retreating to Richmond. General Howard, in command of the right wing, was told by junior officers that the woods behind him were filling up with Confederate soldiers, but he had heard from headquarters that the Confederates were retreating, so he laughed at his officers. They were imagining things, he said. Those woods were too thick for an army to get through.

By late afternoon the six-mile column, still hidden among the trees, had reached its destination and was halted while Jackson positioned the men properly, moved the artillery, and prepared for the attack. He had already been to the top of a hill where he had seen the enemy—unsuspecting, at ease before their campfires. Some were playing cards, some preparing the evening meal, some simply loafing. Jackson kept the movements of his men as quiet as possible and at last everything seemed in order. He took his watch out of his pocket; it was 5:15. He nodded at General Rodes who was to lead the attack.

"You can go forward," Jackson said.

A bugler blew the call for a charge. Then out of the woods Jackson's army sprang with a blood-curdling rebel yell that so frightened the wild creatures of the woods they streamed into the clearing. The first thing the Yankees saw were terrified rabbits, squirrels, pheasants, and other woodland creatures running and flying toward them. Then the Confederate soldiers, still yelling like demons, plunged down upon them. Leaving everything behind, the Yankees joined the rabbits and squirrels and raced for their lives.

The Confederates pursued. Jackson had told his men that no matter what happened, they must keep pursuing—drive the enemy to Chancellorsville and even beyond. Right into the river, if possible. This was the night to end the war. Jackson, himself, was like a man possessed, filled with a sense of infinite power, in love with the moment, in league with God. He kept raising his right arm, perhaps out of habit to let the blood drain into his body, perhaps in prayer to indicate that he and God were doing this together. Occasionally one of the officers would call to Jackson, congratulating him on the success of the operation. Without a word, Jackson would simply point a finger to heaven to show where the credit belonged.

In the vast confusion of the chase, the Confederates had to stop from time to time to re-form; meanwhile the Union army, with reinforcements from Chancellorsville, began to take a stand. But it was growing dark. In war, the sun seemed either to stay up longer than anyone wanted it to or to go down sooner. This night it abandoned the two armies while they were at a critical phase of their conflict. With just one more hour of daylight, Jackson said, he could accomplish miracles. But light or not, he refused to let anything interfere with his plans. "Push on," he told his men; there would be a night attack.

While the Confederate units, cut off from each other in the wild scramble, were trying to sort themselves out in the darkness, Stonewall Jackson and several of his staff rode down the road to study the situation. Jackson was within 2,000 yards of Chancellorsville when one of his staff asked if he really thought he should be where he was.

"The danger is all over," Jackson replied shortly. In any case, hadn't he always been safe? Tonight nothing would stop him. Although he could see that the Yankees were no longer on the run, he was determined that this time he would not simply defeat the enemy; he would, as he had always dreamed, destroy it.

It was nine o'clock. Scattered shot could be heard here and there; voices of men lost from their units called out. Behind fences, crouched by the side of the road, bent low in the fields, were hundreds of dim or invisible figures. Union or Confederate—who could tell? The moon came out, aloof, serene, indifferent as always, and the whippoorwills sang. Any soldier who survived the Battle of Chancellorsville never forgot how the whippoorwills carried on that night, how they persisted—"whip-poor-will, whip-poor-will"—on and on, faster and faster, without stopping for breath, as if they were competing in their private springtime, as if men and war didn't exist.

Stonewall Jackson, having discovered the position of the enemy on the right of the road, was returning from his scouting mission when suddenly a volley of shots rang out from his left. A nervous North Carolina unit had heard horses going by and took for granted that they were Union cavalry. One of Jackson's officers tried to set them straight. He jumped to the ground and ran toward the shooting. "Cease firing!" he shouted. "You are firing into your own men!"

A North Carolina officer thought this was a Yankee trick. "It's a lie!" he cried. "Pour it into them, boys!"

A whole line of North Carolinians fired into the night. One bullet hit Stonewall Jackson in his right hand. Two more lodged in his left arm. A staff member caught the reins of Little Sorrel; others lifted Stonewall to the ground, helped him to a spot under a tree, applied a tourniquet to his bleeding arm, sent for a doctor, and eventually got him on a litter while the battle continued on all sides—confused but persistent. Jackson endured a nightmare of pain while the litter was moved slowly over rough ground, dropped once, righted, and carried through falling enemy bullets to an ambulance wagon. Miles of bumpy road lay ahead but at midnight Stonewall was finally at a field hospital and with him was his friend, Dr. McGuire.

They were going to give him chloroform, Dr. McGuire explained, so they could examine his arm. If they found it necessary to amputate, should they go ahead?

"Yes, certainly," Jackson replied. "Dr. McGuire, do for me whatever you think best." Jackson had suffered without complaint and spoken courteously throughout his ordeal, and the idea of losing an arm could be no great shock. After every battle, around every field hospital, there were hundreds of men who had lost an arm or a leg, for doctors would amputate rather than risk gangrene, for which there was no cure.

They had to amputate now. The doctors found the bones in Jackson's upper arm shattered and an artery had been severed. There was no choice; they removed the arm two inches below the shoulder.

The next morning Stonewall felt much improved. He drank coffee, dozed through much of that day and the next, but on Monday, May 4th, orders came from headquarters to move General Jackson to a safer spot. The fighting was not over. Stonewall thought of friends who lived south of Fredericksburg; they had a small office building on their property similar to the one he had used at the Corbins'. It turned out to be a convenient and comfortable spot and indeed Jackson appeared to be making a successful recovery here. Of course he had that cold that he'd caught the night before the surprise attack, but that was only an annoyance.

On May 6th he looked forward to the arrival of Anna and Julia the next day. Anna would be pleased, he thought, to hear the message he'd received from General Lee. "Tell him," Lee had said, "to make haste and get well, and come back to me as soon as he can. He has lost his left arm; but I have lost my right arm."

That night Stonewall woke up with severe pain in his right side, but he wasn't concerned. He was used to abdominal upsets and knew just what to do for them. No need to wake the doctor, he told his servant Jim. Just bring him a cold, wet towel and place it over his stomach. Jim did as he was told but this time the wet towel brought no relief. The pain became more intense and at daylight Jackson called for Dr. McGuire.

As soon as the doctor saw Jackson, he recognized what had happened. Jackson had developed pneumonia. It was not uncommon for pneumonia to follow an operation, but it was distressing, for he'd seemed to be doing so well. Of course he'd had a cold and the wet towel did not help. It was obvious to Anna, who arrived later in the day, that his condition was serious, but Stonewall, slipping in and out of the delirium, was sure he'd recover. He would be better the next morning, he said. He would not die; God had more work for him to do.

By Sunday, May 10th, it was clear that Stonewall would not live through the day. In his moments of delirium, he was still directing battles, telling

General Hill to move his troops this way and that, urging his men forward. Actually, his last battle had been won during his illness. General Lee had driven Hooker to the river, left him there, gone to Fredericksburg, defeated those Yankees, and returned to find Hooker already across the river on the Union side. With this victory, the southern struggle was at the peak of its success and Old Jack, thirty-nine years old, was its unlikely hero. As it turned out, perhaps this was exactly the right moment for Stonewall Jackson to leave the scene, for certainly he did not doubt that the south would win the war. His peculiar talents, which could never have been realized without just the right combination of time and circumstance, had been pushed to their limits.

So on Sunday morning when Julia told him the doctors said he would die that day, he nodded. The hard knot inside seemed to loosen. "My wish is fulfilled," he said. "I have always desired to die on Sunday."

There were a few more hours of delirium while the clock on the mantelpiece clicked, clicked, clicked. At three-fifteen Stonewall's face relaxed and he seemed suddenly overcome by a sense of peace.

"Let us cross over he river," he said, "and rest under the shade of the trees."

Like his hero, Wolfe at Quebec, he might as well have said, "I die content."

Epilogue

After Chancellorsville, General Lee, thinking that victory was within his grasp, began planning for what turned out to be the Battle of Gettysburg where the tide of the war turned against the south. After his defeat, Lee said he would never have been beaten if Stonewall had been there, but in the long run President Lincoln was right. The war was a question of arithmetic. Lincoln finally found his winning general, and when enough bodies had been piled up and a whole generation of young men had all but been wiped out, the war ended.

Jackson had been dead two years when the south surrendered. He had been given a hero's funeral, first in Richmond where 20,000 people watched the procession, his hearse drawn by four white horses and accompanied by troops marching with reversed arms. Later in Lexington his casket was taken by cadets and placed in his old classroom for viewing. Old Jack was a legend now.

Years later at a reunion of Confederate veterans in Richmond, a group of gray-haired men were found sleeping on the ground around Stonewall's statue in Capitol Square. They were among the few survivors of the old Stonewall Brigade. "We were his boys," one veteran explained, "and we wanted to sleep with the Old Man just once more."

Bibliography

The quotes used in this book were taken from the following sources.

Bradford, Ned, ed. *Battles and Leaders of the Civil War*. New York: Appleton-Century-Crofts, 1956.

Casler, John. *Four Years in the Stonewall Brigade*. Guthrie, Okla.: State Capital Press, 1893.

Catton, Bruce. *Glory Road*. New York: Doubleday & Co., 1952.

Chambers, L. *Stonewall Jackson*. New York: William Morrow & Co., 1959.

Chase, William C. *The Story of Stonewall Jackson*. Atlanta, Ga.: D. E. Luther Co., 1901.

Clopton, J. J. *The True Stonewall Jackson*. Baltimore, Md.: Ruths' Sons, Printers, 1913.

Commager, H. S., ed. *The Blue and the Gray*. Indianapolis, Ind.: Bobbs-Merrill Co., 1950.

Cook, Roy Bird. *The Family and Early Life of Stonewall Jackson and the Old Stonewall Brigade*. Charlottseville, Va.: University Press of Virginia, 1954.

Dabney, Robert L. *Life and Campaigns of Lieutenant General Thomas J. Jackson*. New York, 1866.

Davis, Burke. *They Called Him Stonewall*. New York: Rinehart & Co., 1954.

Douglas, Henry Kyd. *I Rode with Stonewall*. Chapel Hill, N.C.: University of N.C. Press, 1940.

Freeman, Douglas S. *Lee's Lieutenants*. New York: Charles Scribner's Sons, 1943.

Goolrick, John. *Historic Fredericksburg*. Fredericksburg, Va., 1922.

Happel, Ralph. *The Last Days of Jackson*. Washington, D.C.: National Park Service, 1971.

Henderson, Col. G. F. R. *Stonewall Jackson and the American Civil War*. Toronto: Longmans, Green & Co., 1949

Hunter, Alexander. *Johnny Reb and Billy Yank*. New York & Washington: Neale Publishing Co., 1905.

Jackson, Mary Anna. *Life and Letters of Stonewall Jackson*. New York: Harper & Bros., 1892.

Kirwan, D., ed. *The Confederacy*. Yonkers, N.Y.: World Book Co., 1959.

Leech, Margaret. *Reveille in Washington*. New York: Harper & Brothers, 1941.

Long, A. L. *Memoirs of Robert E. Lee*. New York, Philadelphia, Washington: J. M Stoddart & Co., 1886.

Long, E. B. *The Civil War Day by Day*. New York: Doubleday & Co., 1971.

Lowenfels, Walter, ed. *Walt Whitman's Civil War*. New York: Alfred A. Knopf, 1960.

Maury, Betty H. "A Confederate Diary." Manuscript, Fredericksburg, Va.

Maury, Dabney H. *Recollections of a Virginian*. London, 1894.

Poore, Ben P. *The Life and Public Services of Ambrose E. Burnside*. Providence, R.I., 1882.

Quin, S. *The History of Fredericksburg*. Richmond, Va.: Hermitage Press, 1908.

Sandburg, Carl. *Abraham Lincoln*. New York: Harper & Brothers, 1954.

Selby, John. *Stonewall Jackson*. London: B. T. Batsford, Ltd., 1968.

Stern, Philip Van Doren. *Soldier Life in the Union & Confederate Armies*. Bloomington, Ind.: Indiana University Press, 1961.

Strode, Hudson. *Jefferson Davis*. New York: Harcourt, Brace & Co., 1951.

Tanner, Rob G. *Stonewall in the Valley*. New York: Doubleday & Co., 1976.

Tate, Allen. *Stonewall Jackson: The Good Soldier*. New York: Minton, Balch & Co., 1928.

Taylor, Richard. *Destruction and Reconstruction*, ed. Charles P. Roland. Waltham, Mass.; Toronto; London: Blaisdell Publishing Co., 1968.

Vandiver, Frank. *Mighty Stonewall*. New York: McGraw-Hill Book Co., 1957.

Wainwright, Charles S. *A Diary of a Battle*, ed. Allan Nevins. New York: Harcourt, Brace & Co., 1962.

Wayland, John W. *Stonewall Jackson's Way*. Staunton, Va.: McClure Publishing Co., 1956.

Wheeler, Richard. *We Knew Stonewall Jackson*. New York: Thomas Y. Crowell, 1977.

Williams, T. Harry. *Lincoln and His Generals*. New York: Alfred A. Knopf, 1952.

Worsham, J. H. *One of Jackson's Foot Calvary*. New York & Washington: Neal Publishing Co., 1912.